Unit 1

Lesson 1

Trace and match.

T0355091
pencil
book
crayons
glue
scissors
eraser

New words

Vocabulary: *pencil, book, eraser, scissors, glue, crayons*

Match and color.

Robot

Superhero

Monster

Doll

Monkey

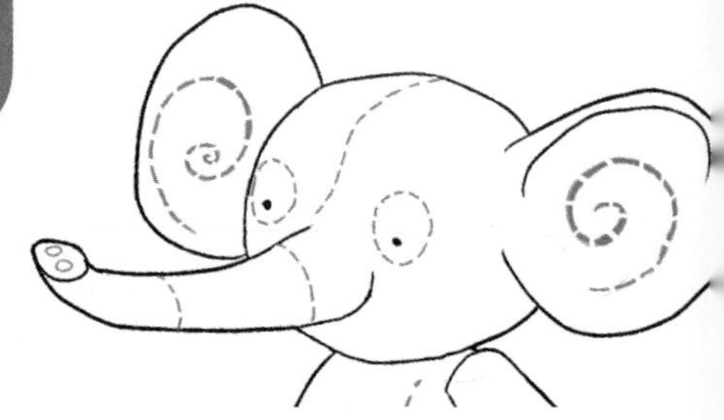

Elephant

Story **Structure:** *I have (a)/(an) …*
Vocabulary: classroom objects

Trace and read. Say *I have (a)/(an) …*

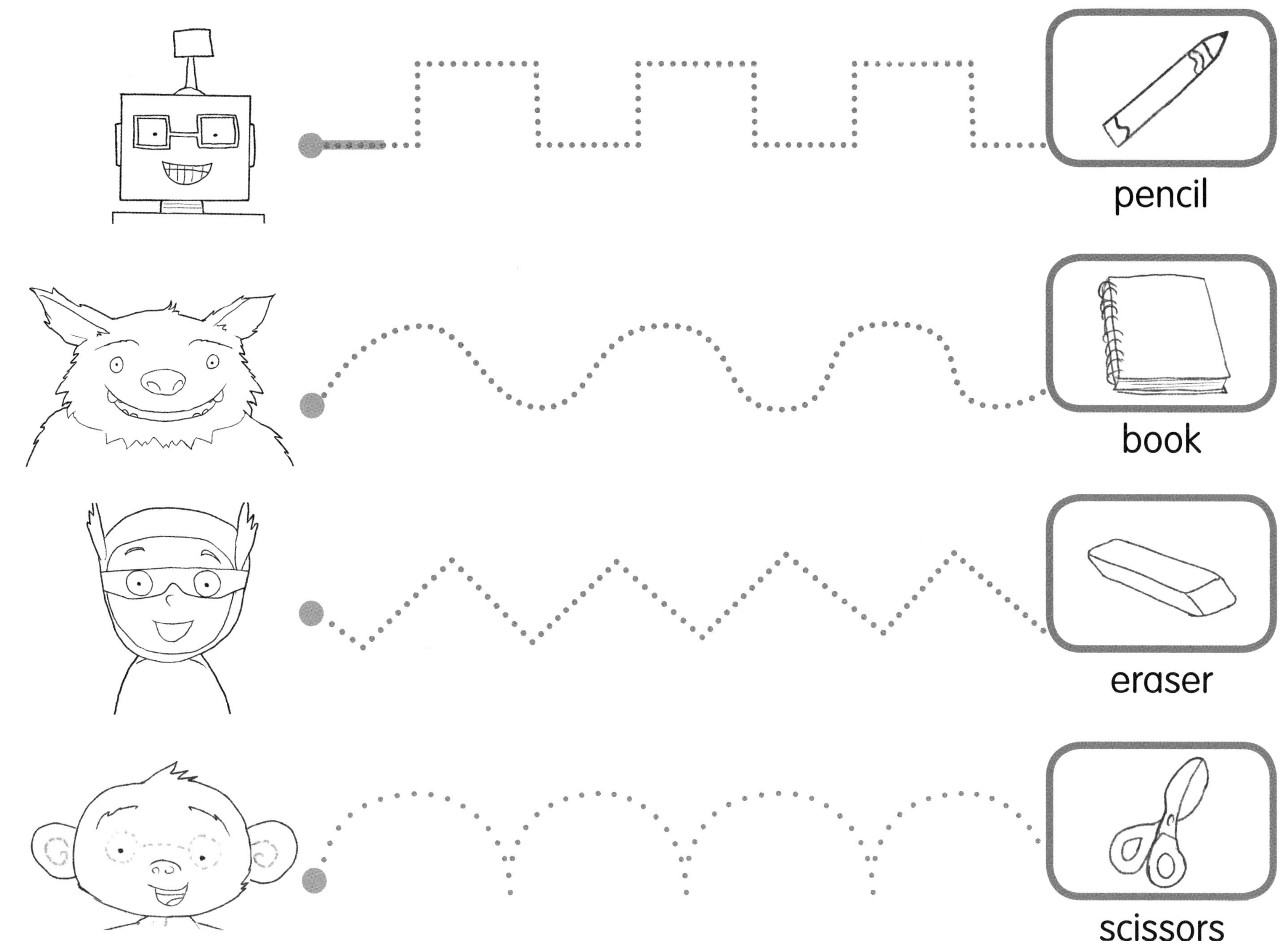
pencil
book
eraser
scissors

Look and circle.

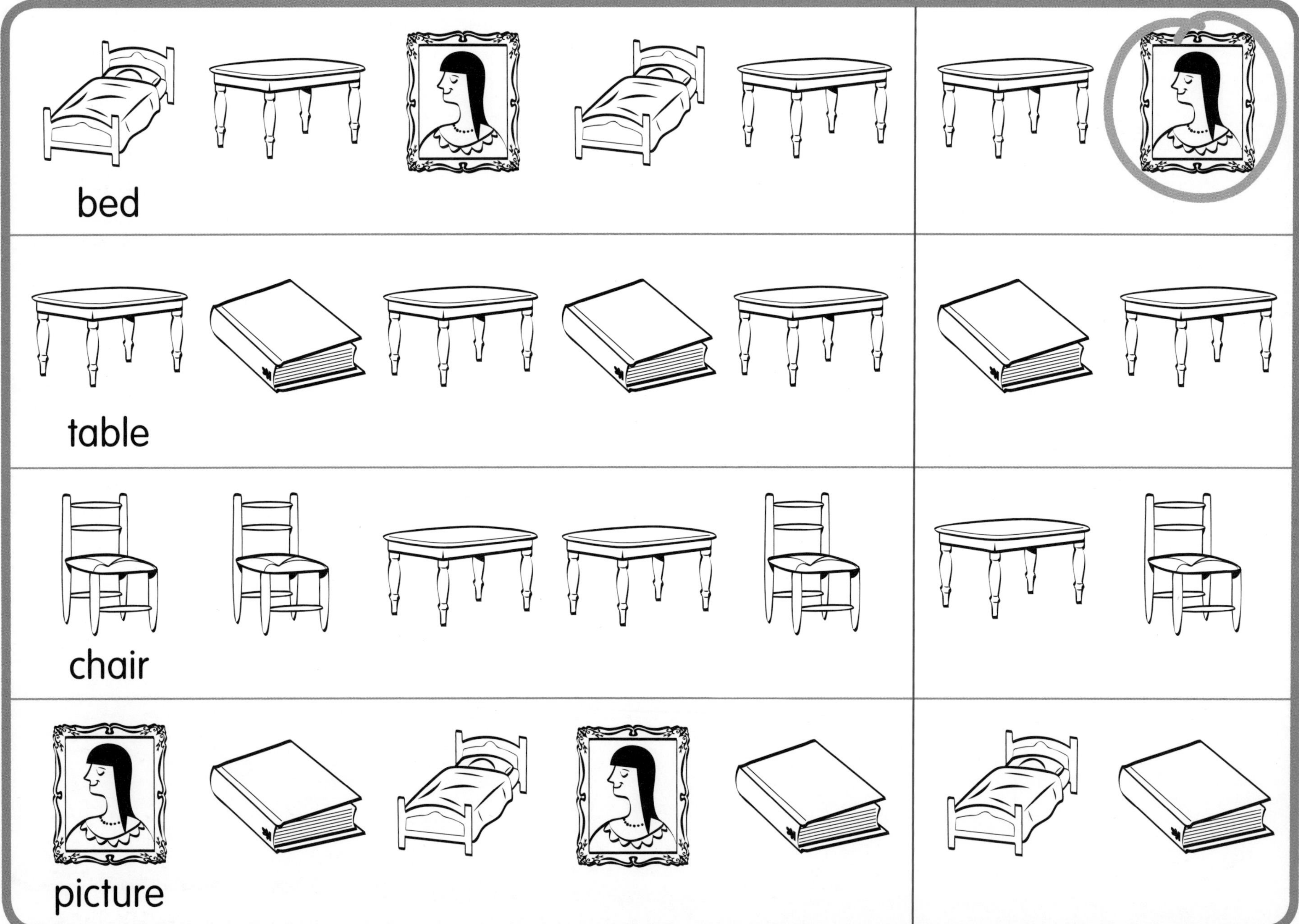
bed
table
chair
picture

Smart topic **Pictures**
Vocabulary: *bed, table, picture, chair*

Count and write.

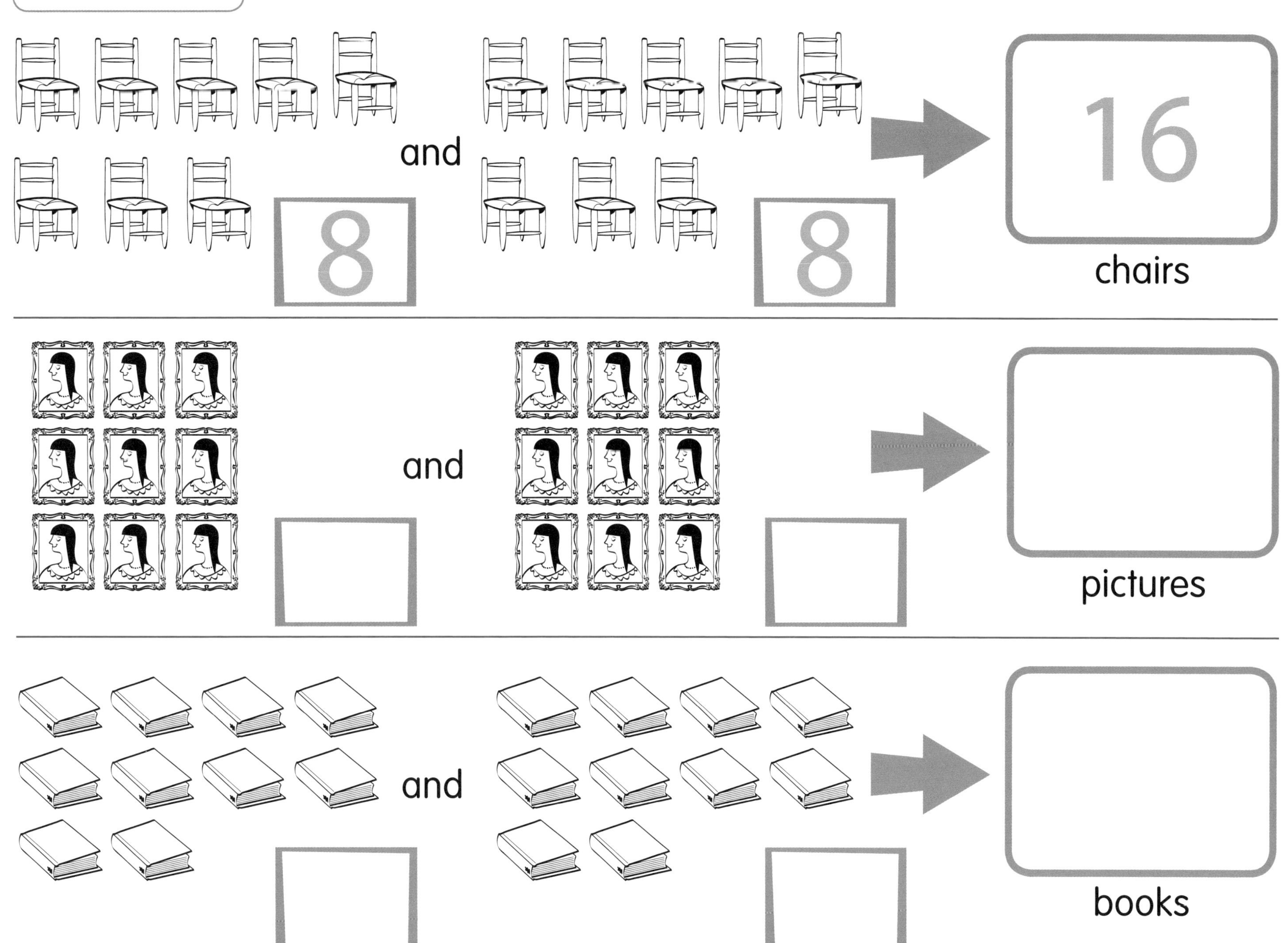
and
8
8
16
chairs
and
pictures
and
books

Look and circle 6 differences in Picture 2.

1

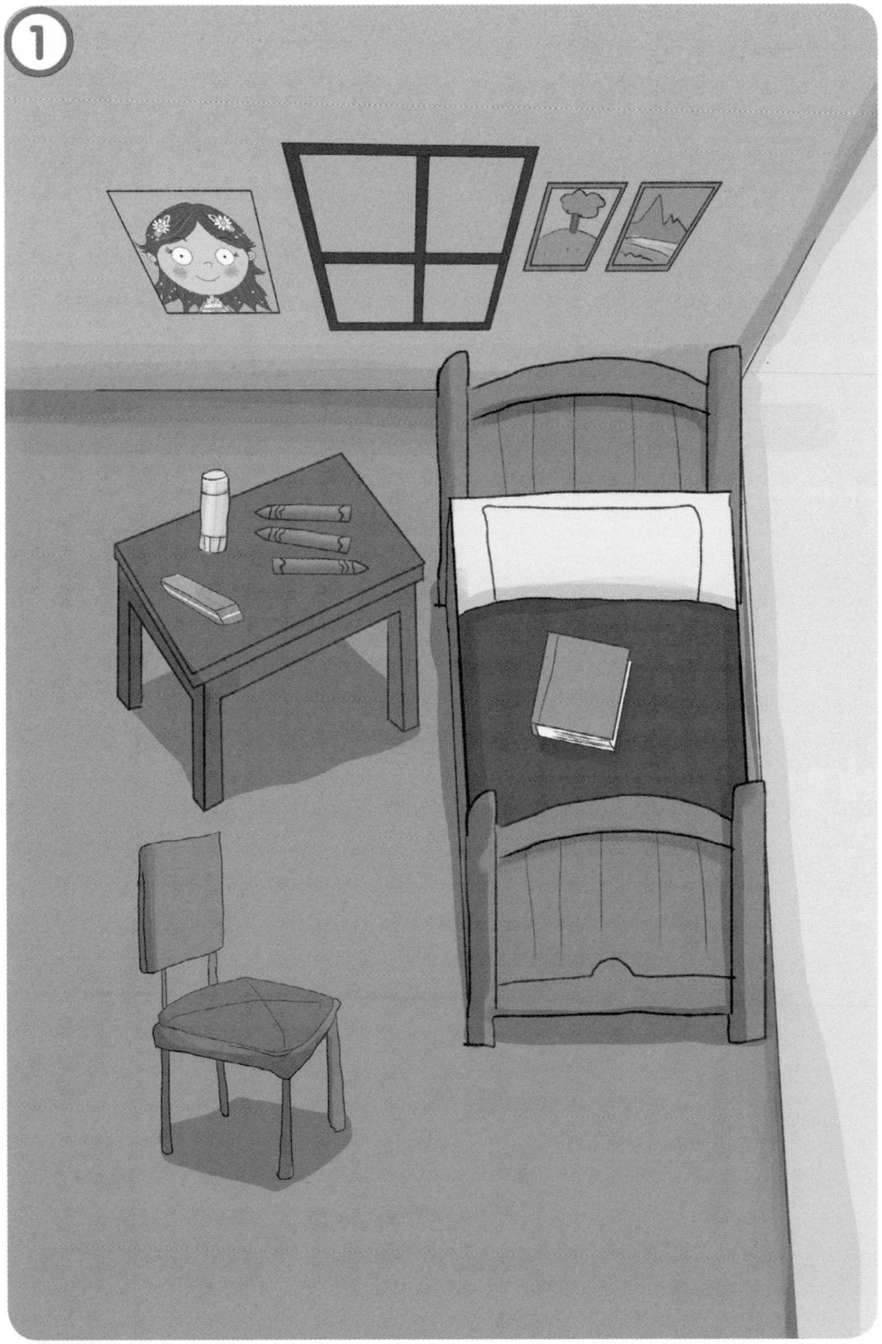

2

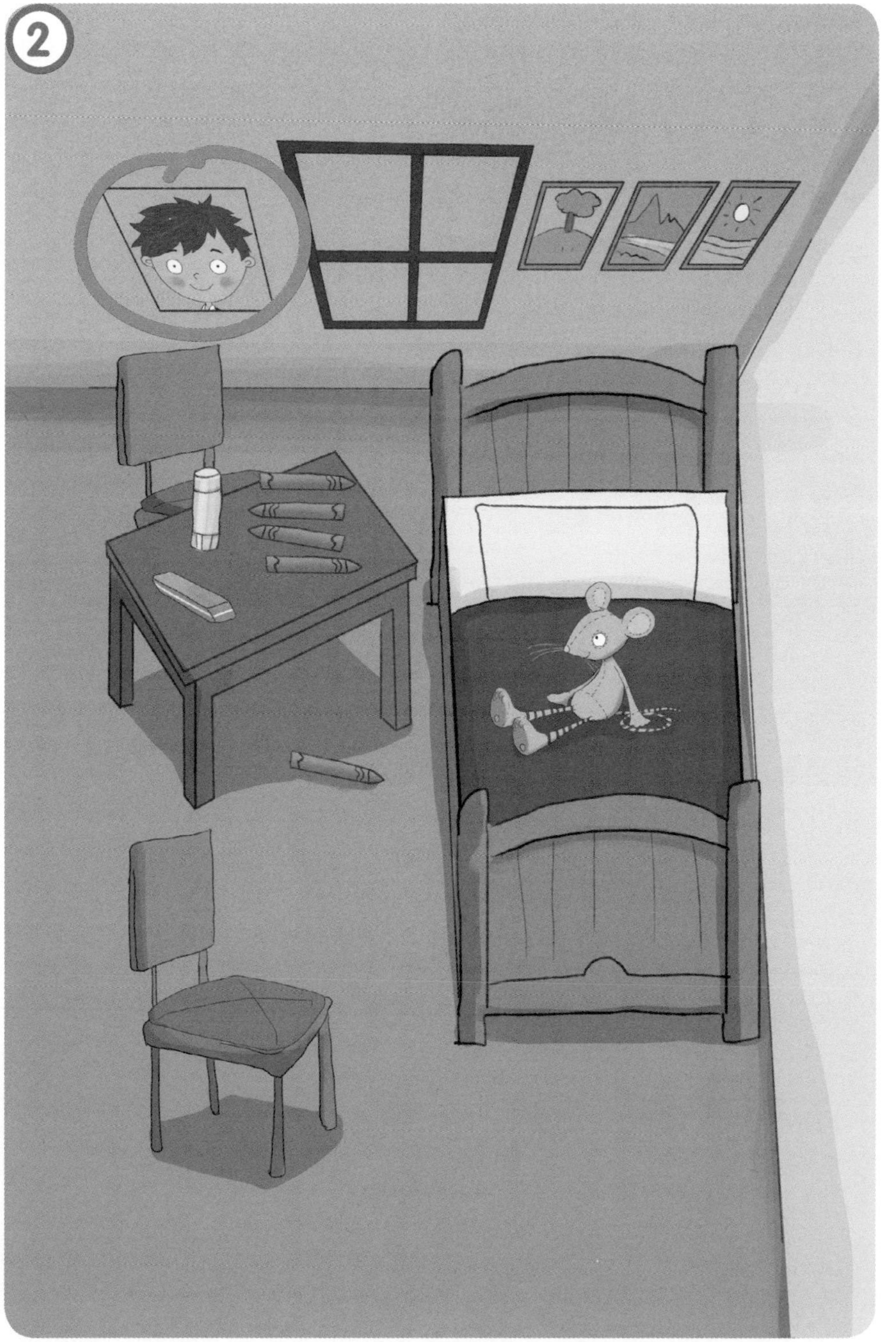

Match and circle. Write the number.

1 2 3
4 5
3

clean the board

1 2 3
4 5 6

1

1 2 3
4 5 6
7 8

2

1 2 3
4 5

3

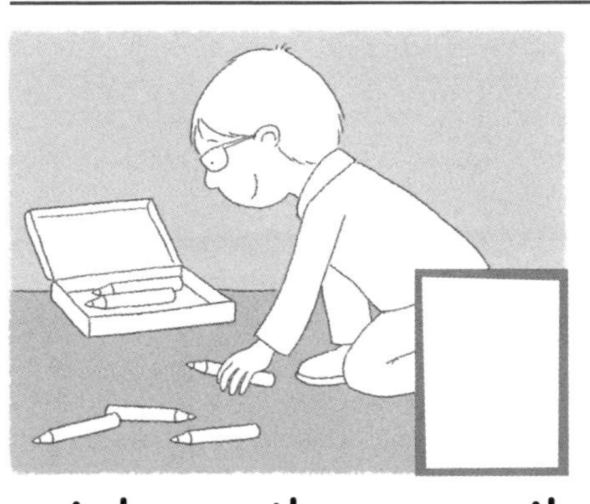

pick up the pencils

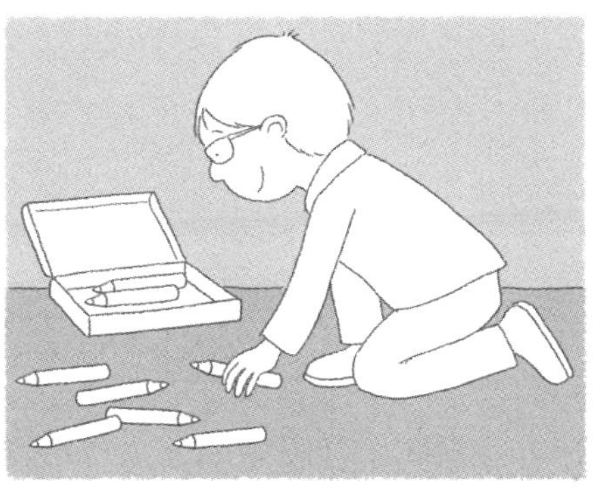

1

2

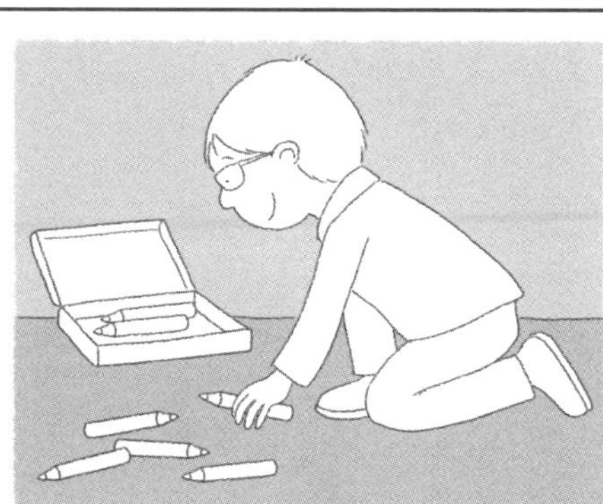

3

collect the books

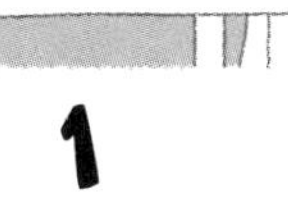

1

2

3

Kindergarten DVD Clean up
Vocabulary: *pencils, board, books*

Read and match. Trace.

I have crayons.

I have a picture.

I have an eraser.

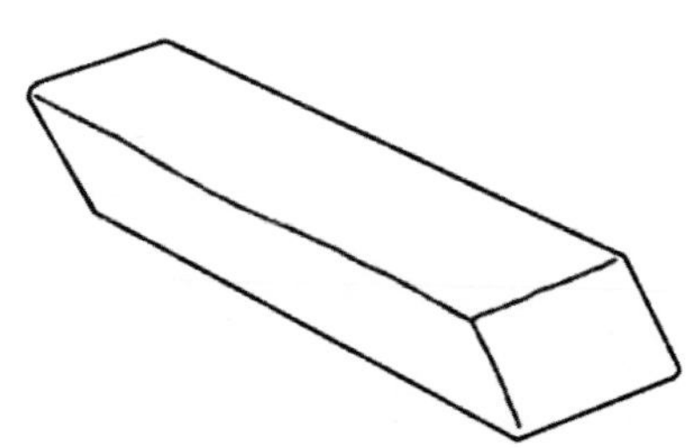

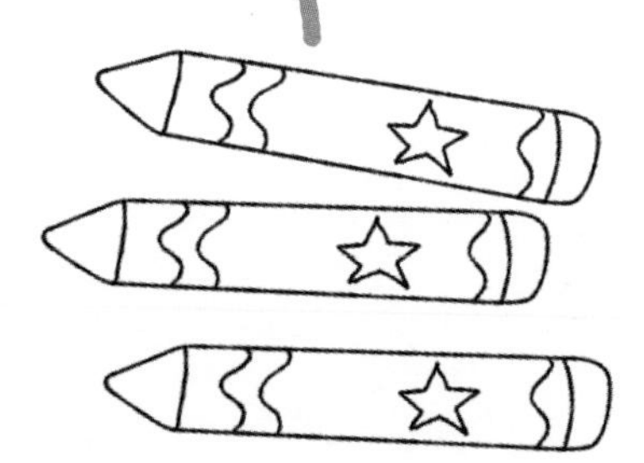

eraser crayons picture

Literacy Tracing whole words
Vocabulary: *crayons, eraser, picture*

Match and write.

20
21
22
23
27
28
25
22
29
24
26

Numeracy **New numbers:** 20, 21, 22, 23, 24, 25, 26, 27, 28, and 29
Counting

Unit
2

Trace and match.

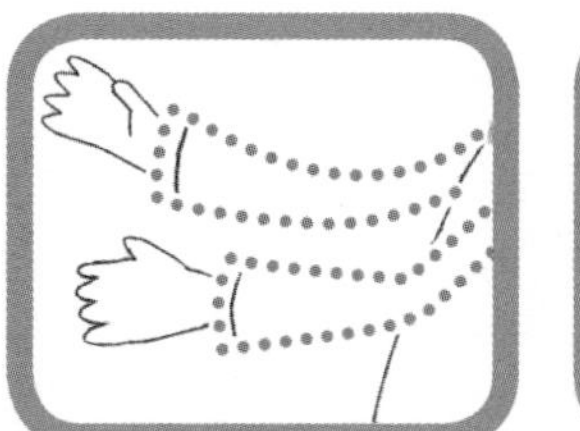

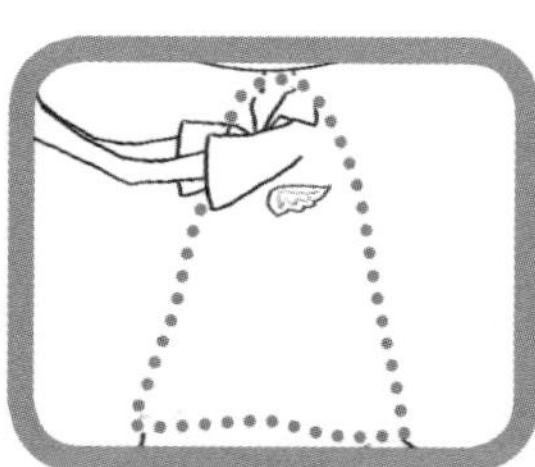
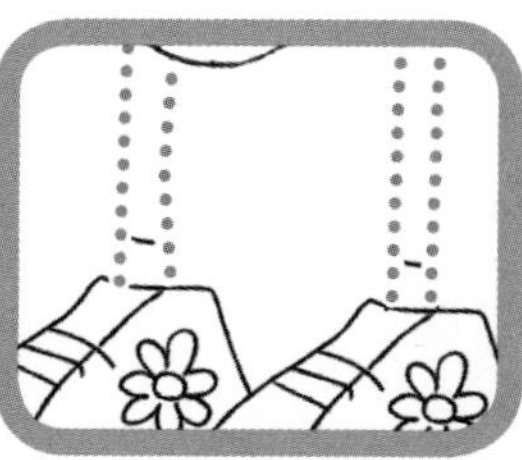

arms head hands feet body legs

New words
Vocabulary: *arms, head, body, legs, feet, hands*

Find and match.

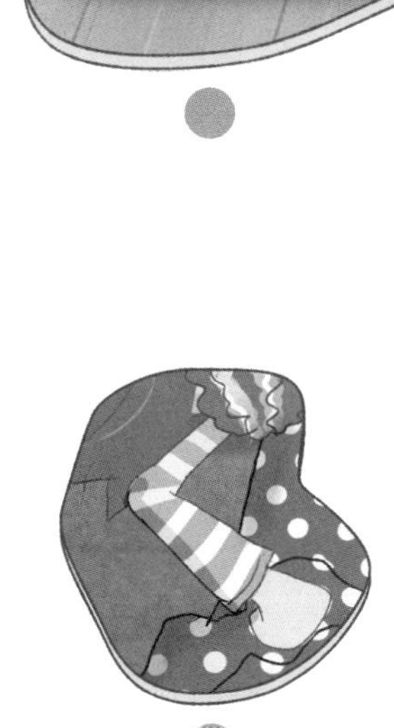

Story **Structure:** *Look at my …*
Vocabulary: parts of the body

Read, trace, and draw. Say *Look at my …*

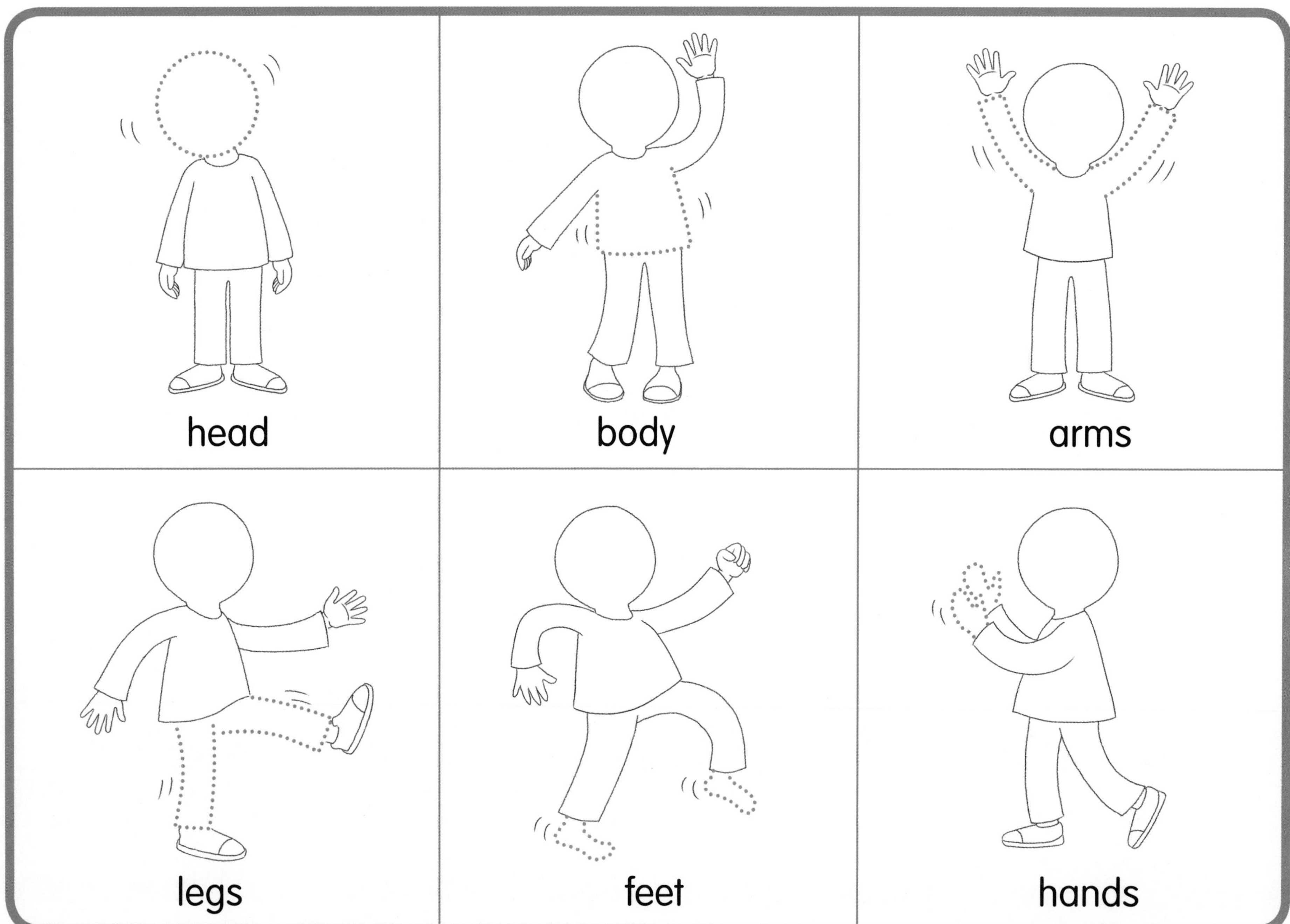
head
body
arms
legs
feet
hands

Story **Structure:** *Look at my …*
Vocabulary: parts of the body

Look and match.

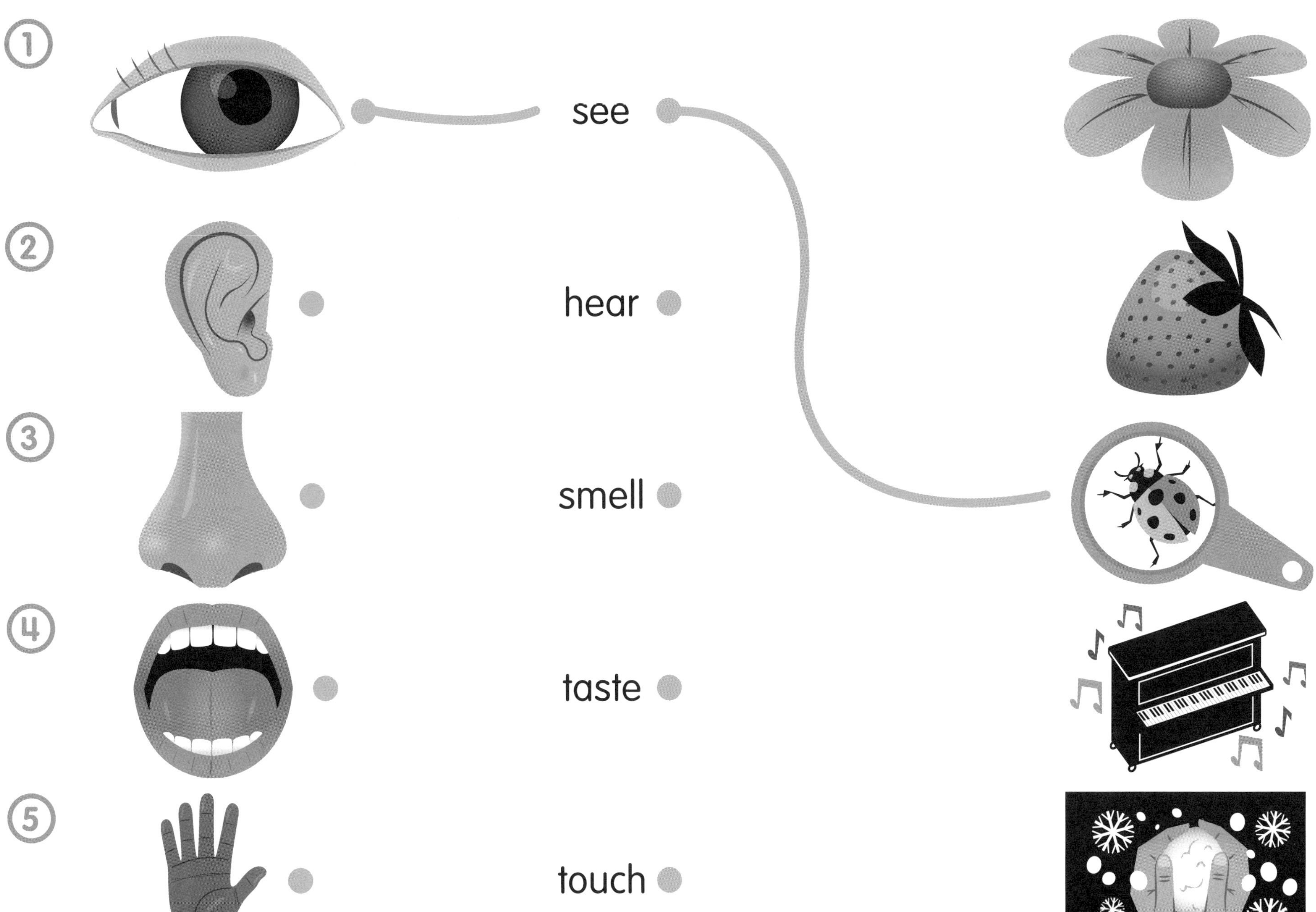
1
2
3
4
5
see
hear
smell
taste
touch

Smart topic Five senses
Vocabulary: *hear, see, smell, taste, touch*

Look and draw.

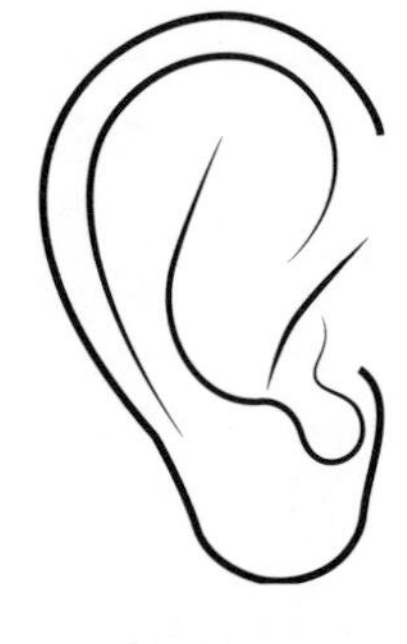	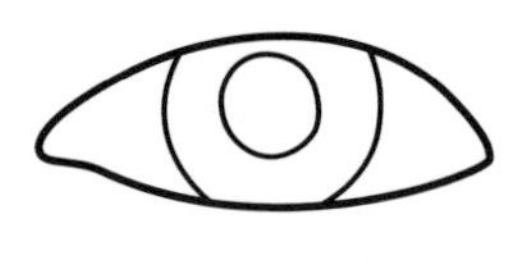	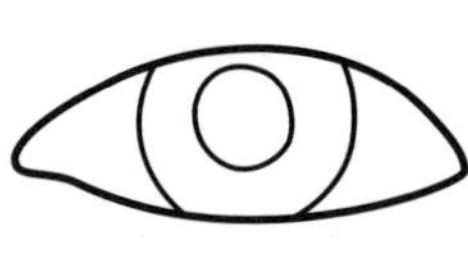	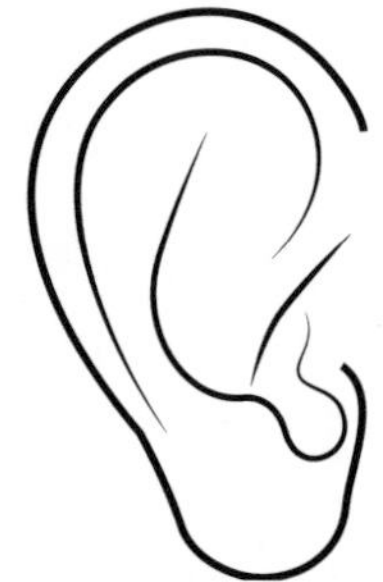	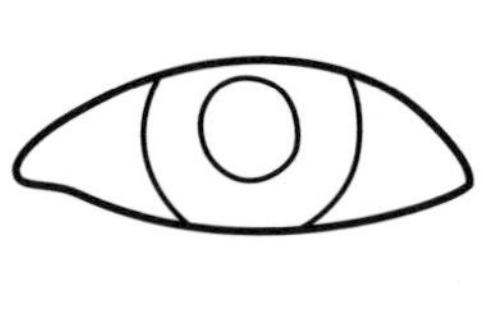	
hear	see	see	hear	see	see
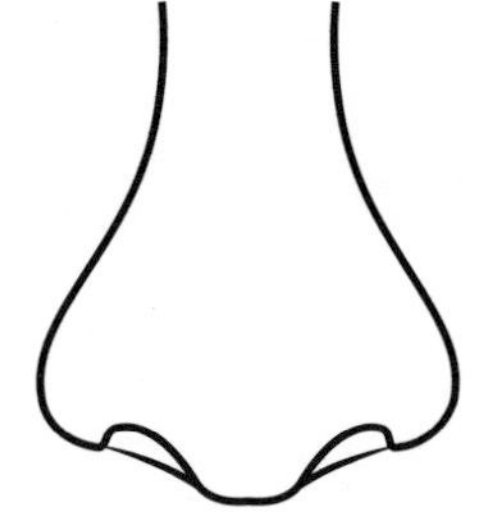 	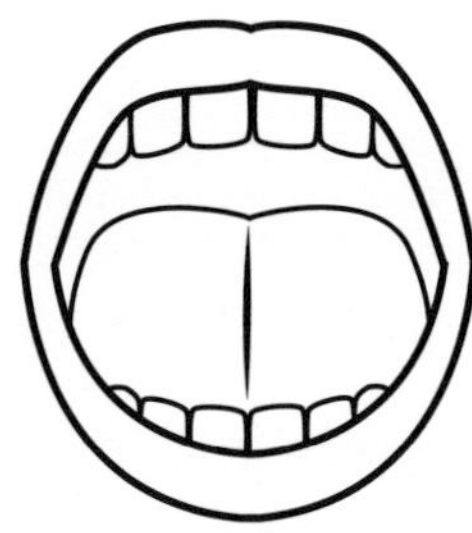	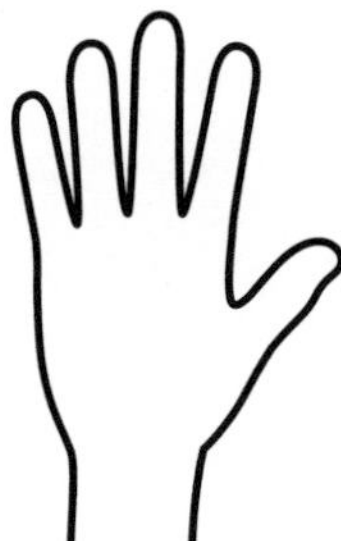	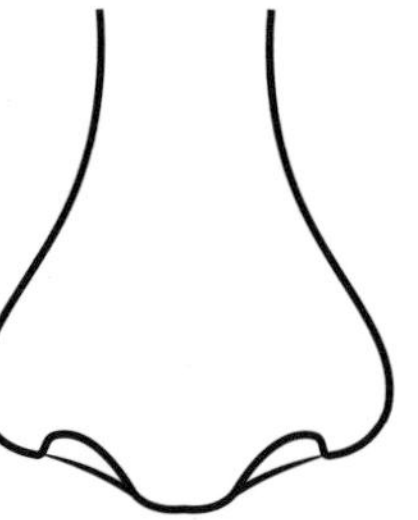	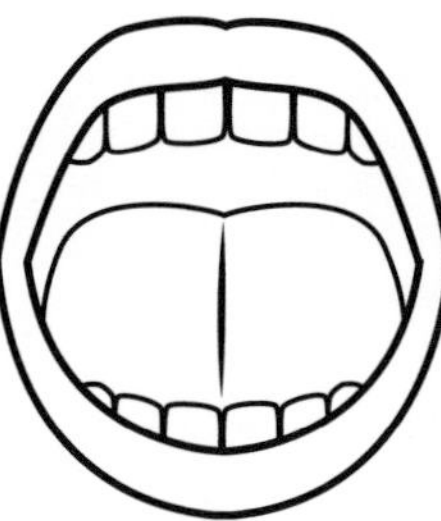	
smell	taste	touch	smell	taste	touch
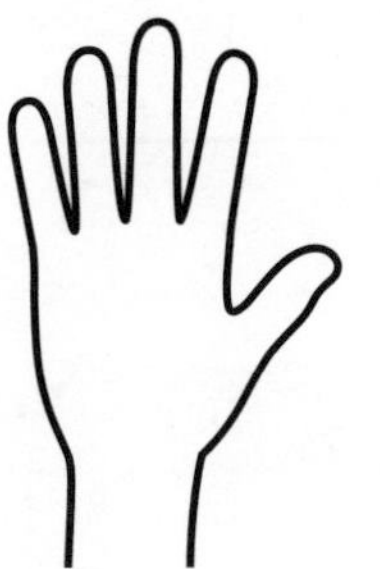	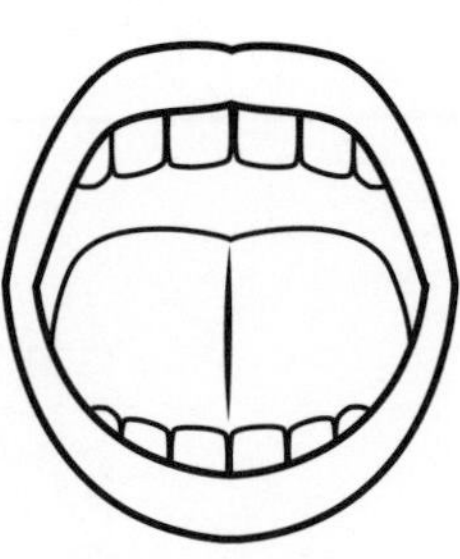	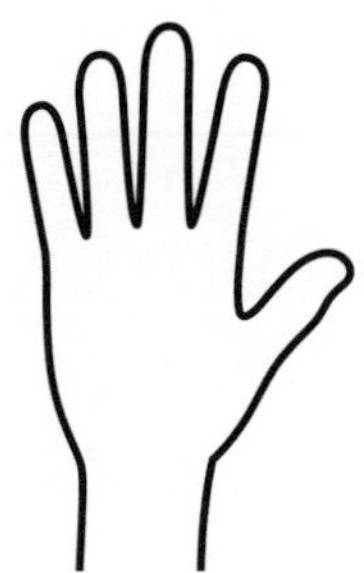	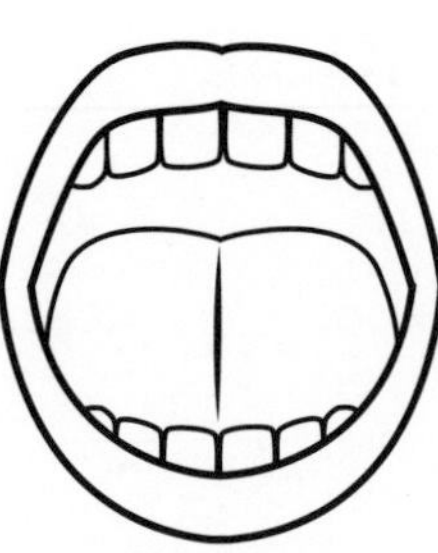	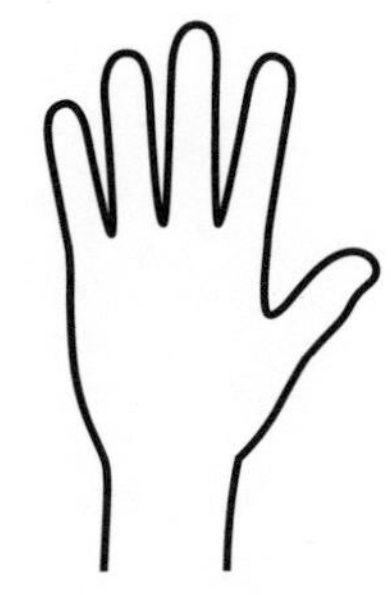	
touch	taste	touch	taste	touch	taste

Look and match. Color.

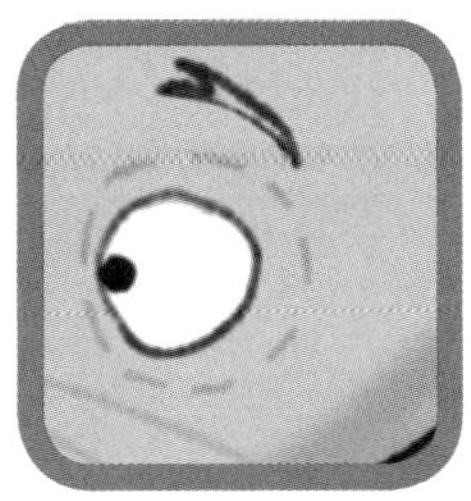
see

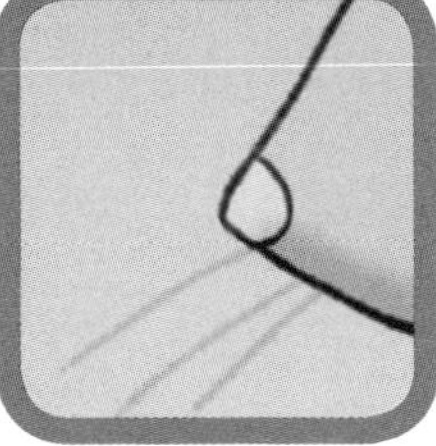
smell

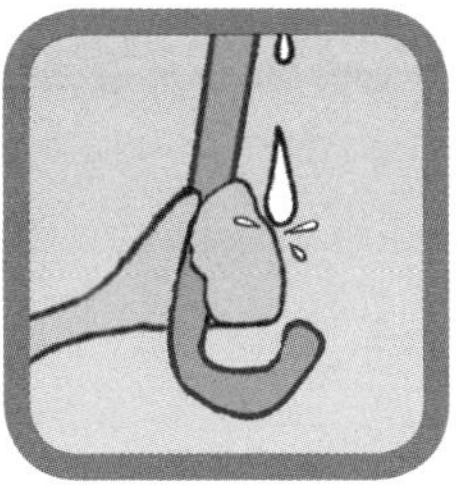
touch

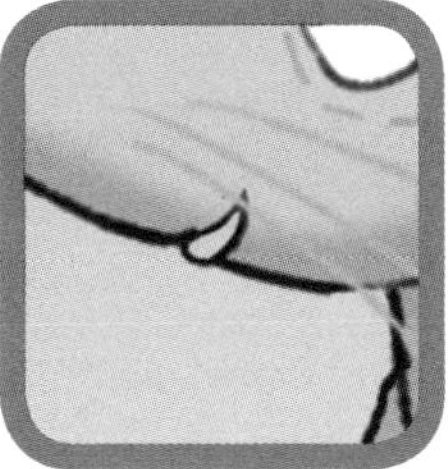
taste

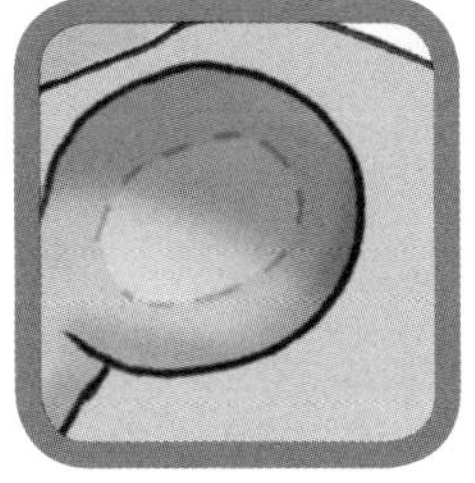
hear

head

hands

arms

body

legs

feet

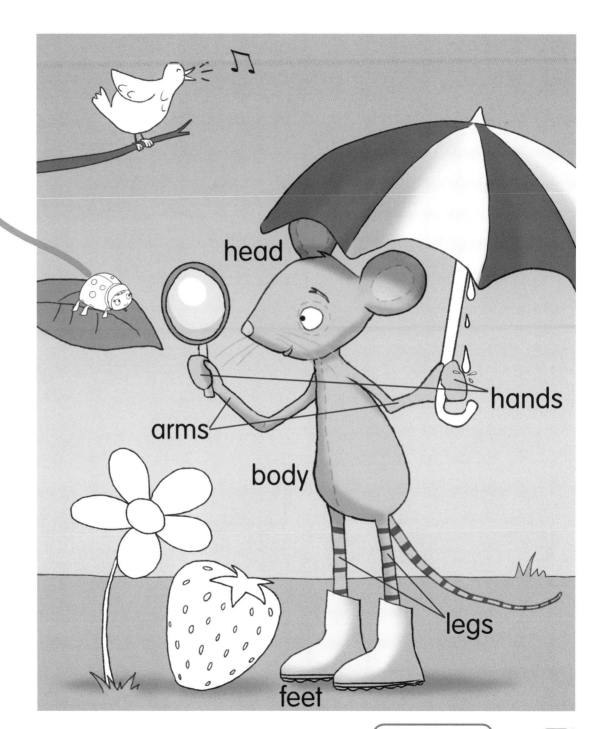

Draw yourself and trace.

stamp your feet

nod your head

bend your legs

Kindergarten DVD **Dance class**
Vocabulary: *stamp your feet, nod your head, bend your legs*

Trace and read.

I can …

see
smell
hear
touch
taste

Literacy Tracing whole words
Vocabulary: *hear, see, smell, taste, touch*

Follow the numbers.

35
32
31
39
33
30
38
31
35
34
36
33
36
39
39
37
38
32

Numeracy **New numbers:** 30, 31, 32, 33, 34, 35, 36, 37, 38, and 39
Counting

Trace and color.

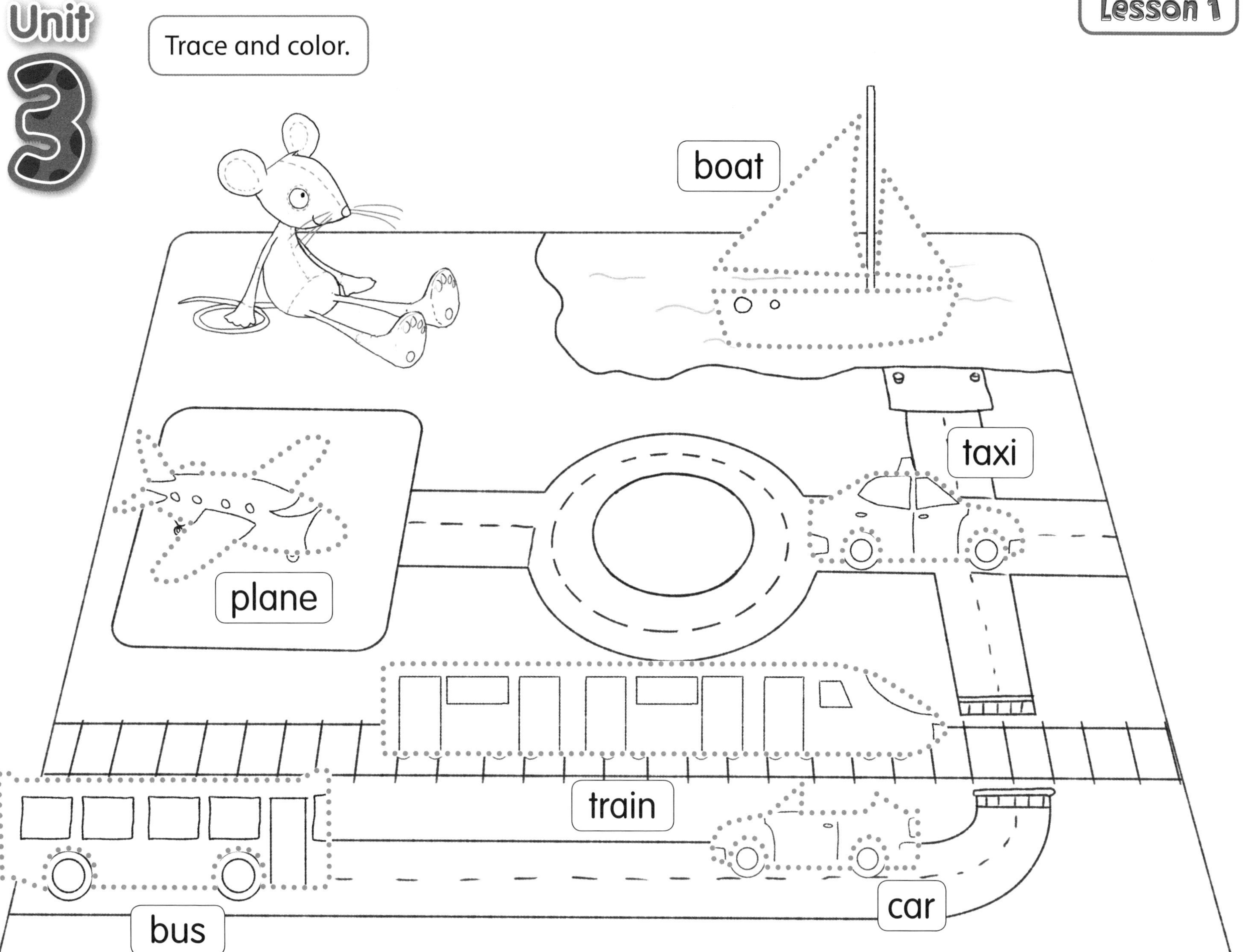
boat
taxi
plane
train
bus
car

New words
Vocabulary: *bus, taxi, car, plane, train, boat*

Look and circle 6 differences in Picture 2.

1

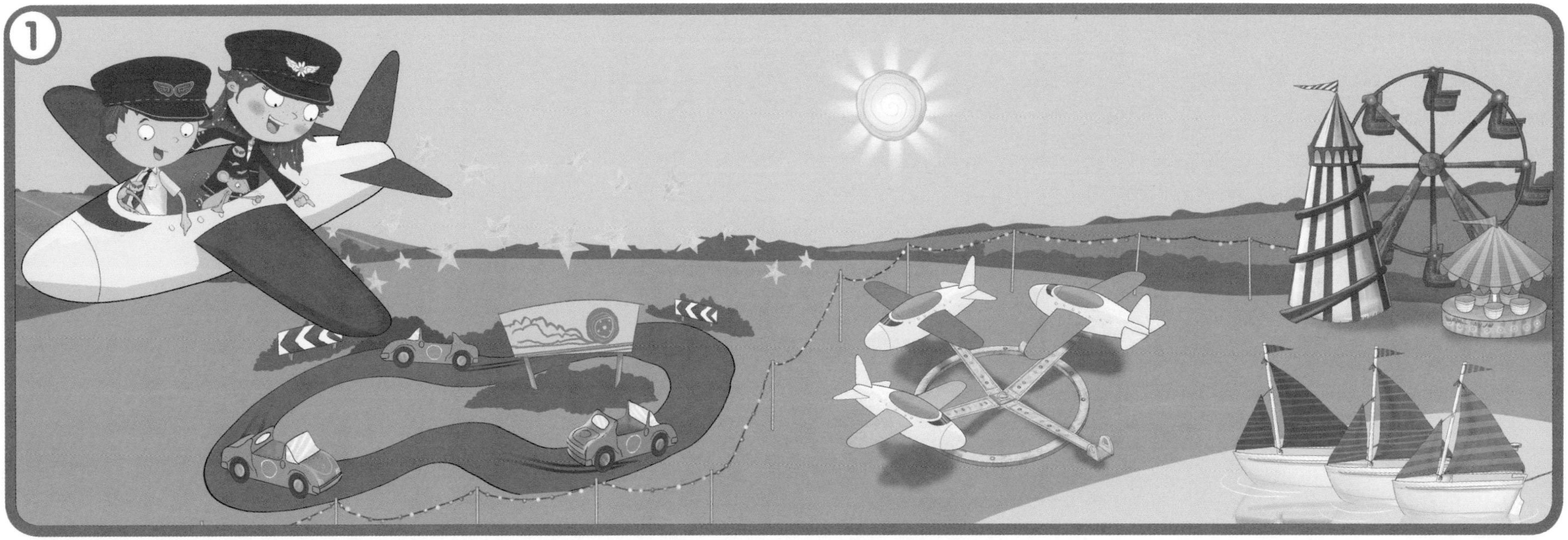

2

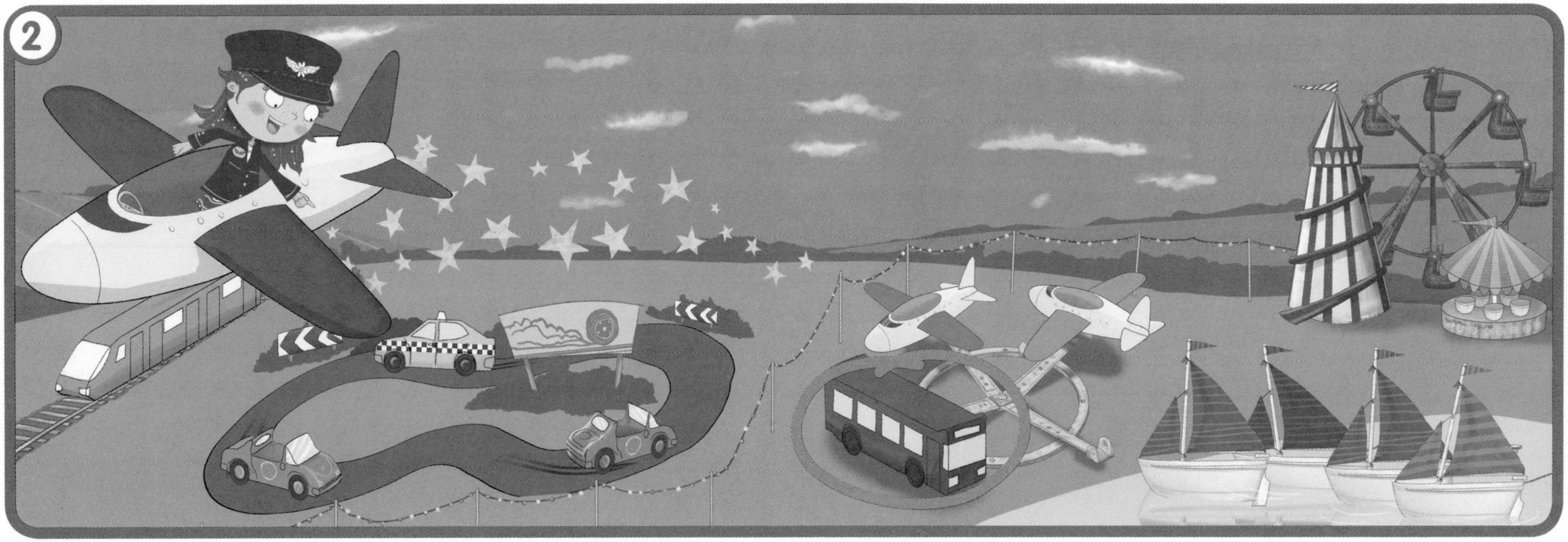

Read and trace. Say *Let's go by …*

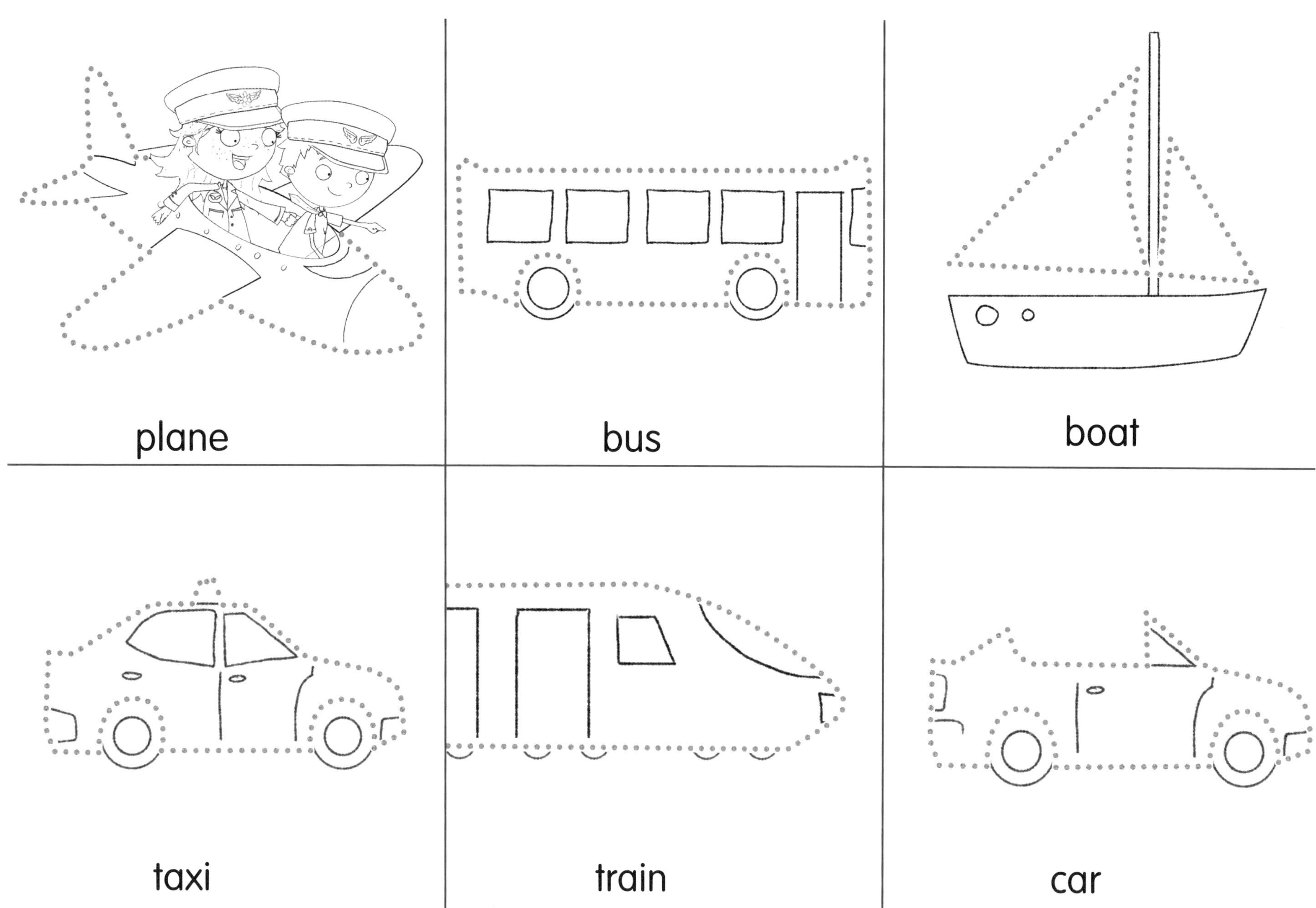
plane
bus
boat
taxi
train
car

Look and match.

plane

boat

car

air

land

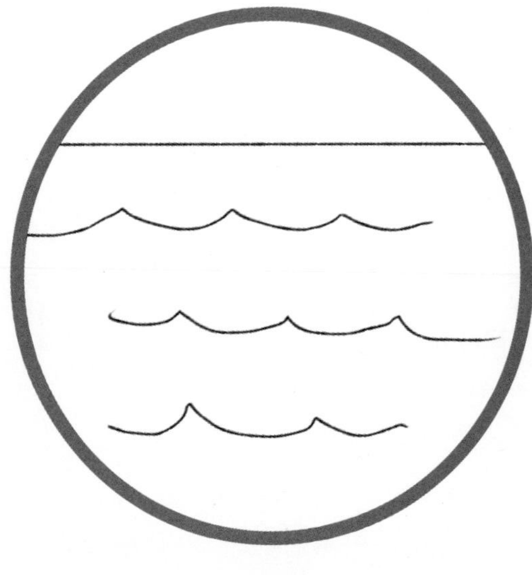

sea

Smart topic **Air, land, and sea**
Vocabulary: *air, land, sea*

Look and draw.

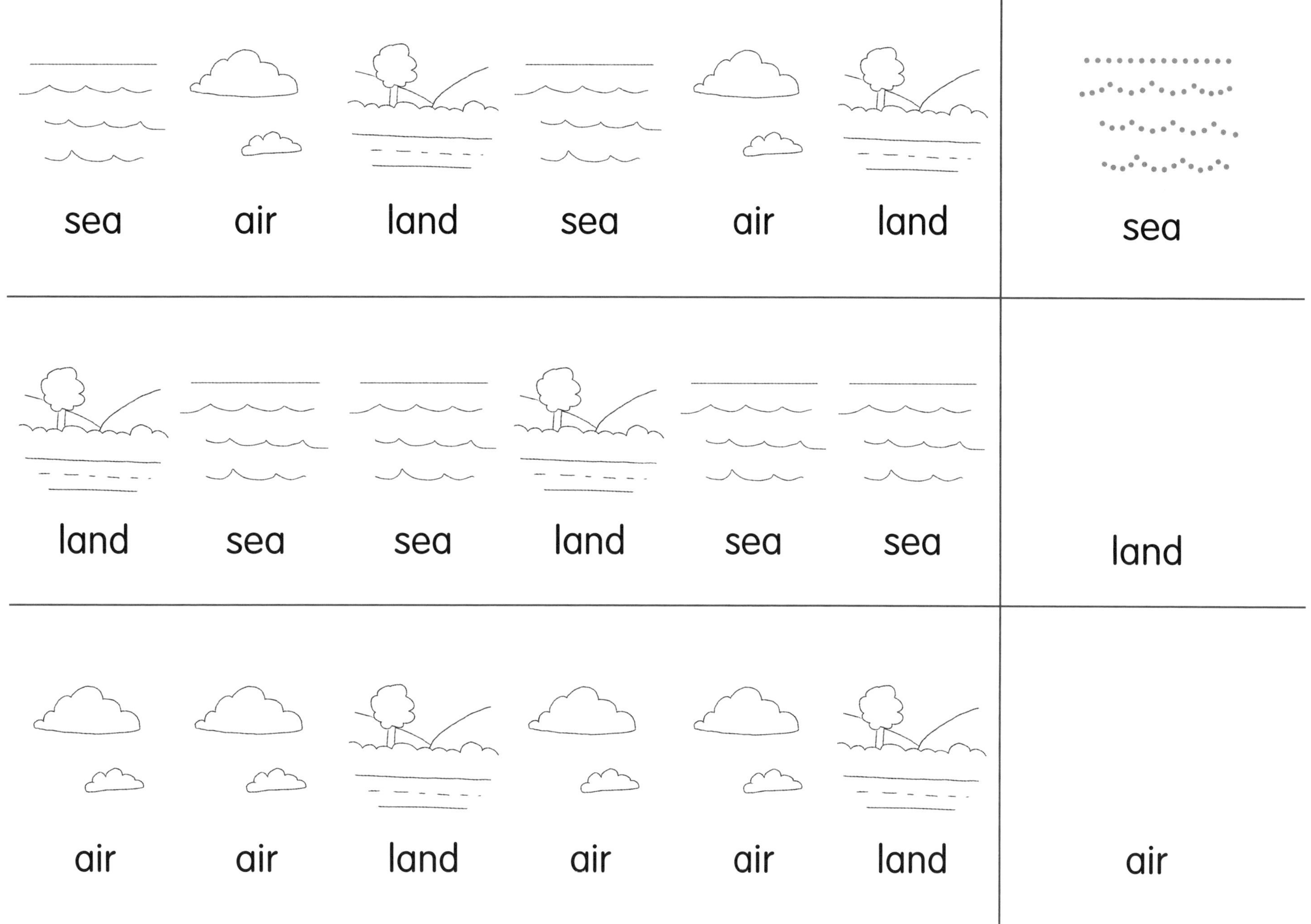
sea
air
land
sea
air
land
sea
land
sea
sea
land
sea
sea
land
air
air
land
air
air
land
air

Look and match.

car

plane

bus

air

land

sea

train

boat

taxi

Follow. Draw yourself getting to kindergarten.

by car
by bike
SCHOOL
walk

Trace. Read and write.

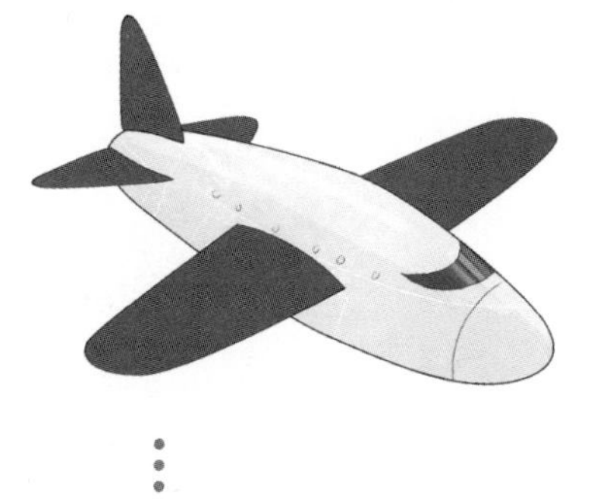

car train plane

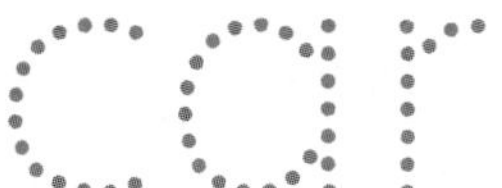

I go by c__ar.

I go by ___rain.

I go by ___lane.

Literacy Tracing whole words; writing initial letters
Vocabulary: vehicles

Write the next number.

42 43

38 

40 

37 

44 

45 

41 

47 

48 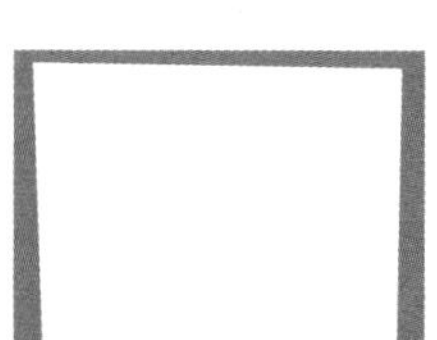

Numeracy **New numbers:** 40, 41, 42, 43, 44, 45, 46, 47, 48, and 49
Counting

Match and trace.

house
window
roof
door
walls
floor

New words
Vocabulary: *house, roof, floor, window, door, walls*

Look and circle 6 differences in Picture 2.

1

2

Read and color. Say *Don't forget the …*

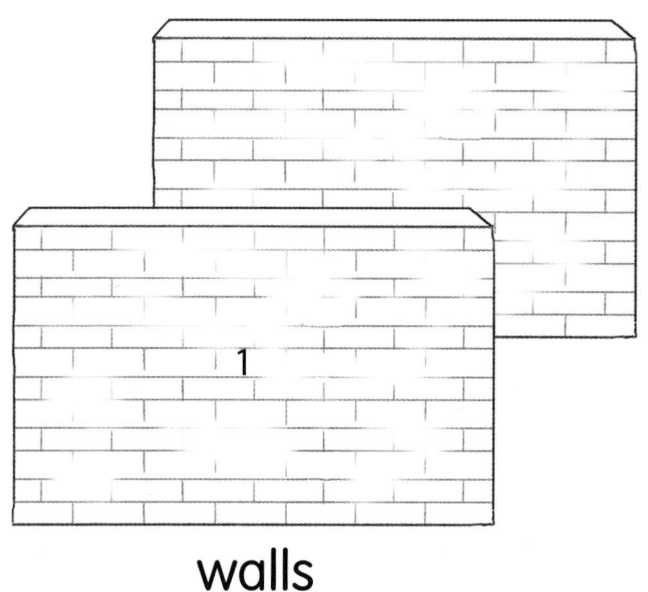
1

walls

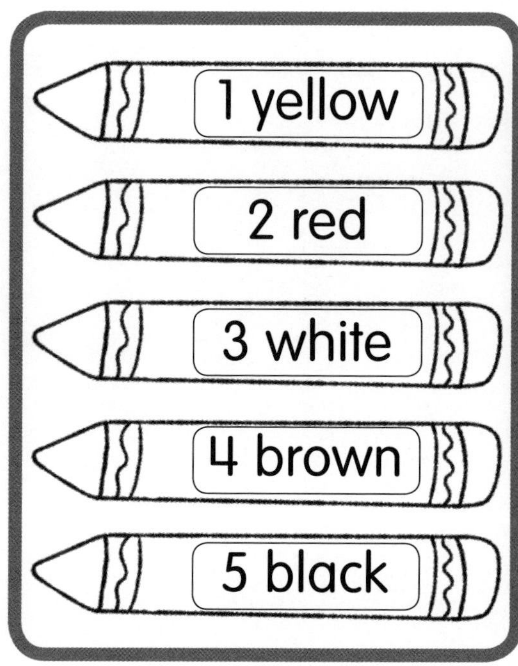
1 yellow
2 red
3 white
4 brown
5 black

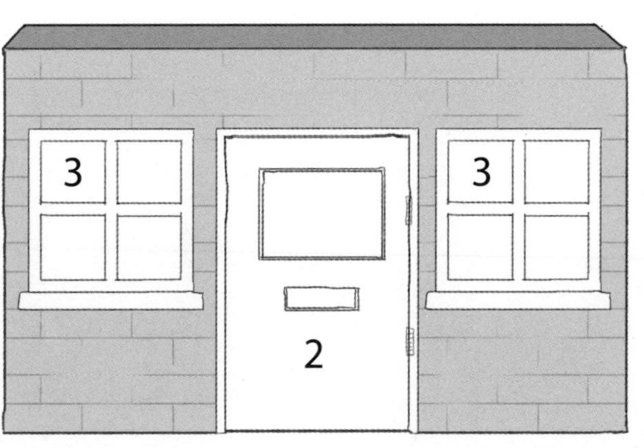
3
3
2

door and windows

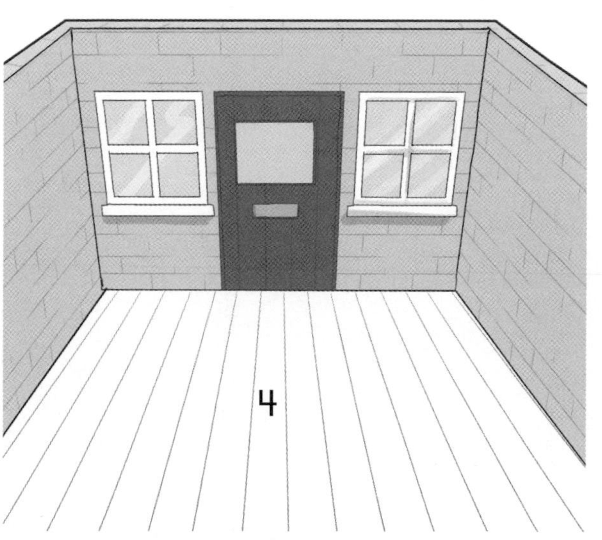
4

floor

5

roof

Story **Structure:** *Don't forget the …*
Vocabulary: parts of a house

Look and match.

wash

play

eat

sleep

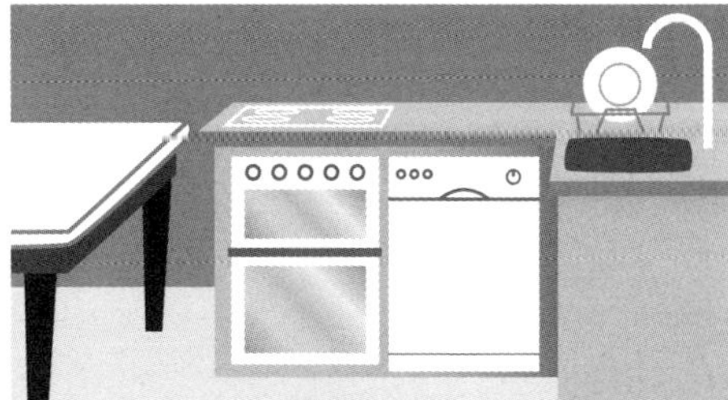
kitchen

bedroom

bathroom

living room

Smart topic Rooms
Vocabulary: *bathroom, kitchen, living room, bedroom*

Look and ✔ or ✘.

bathroom

eat ✘

wash ✔

kitchen

sleep ☐

eat ☐

living room

wash ☐

play ☐

bedroom

sleep ☐

wash ☐

Connect the dots. Draw your family.

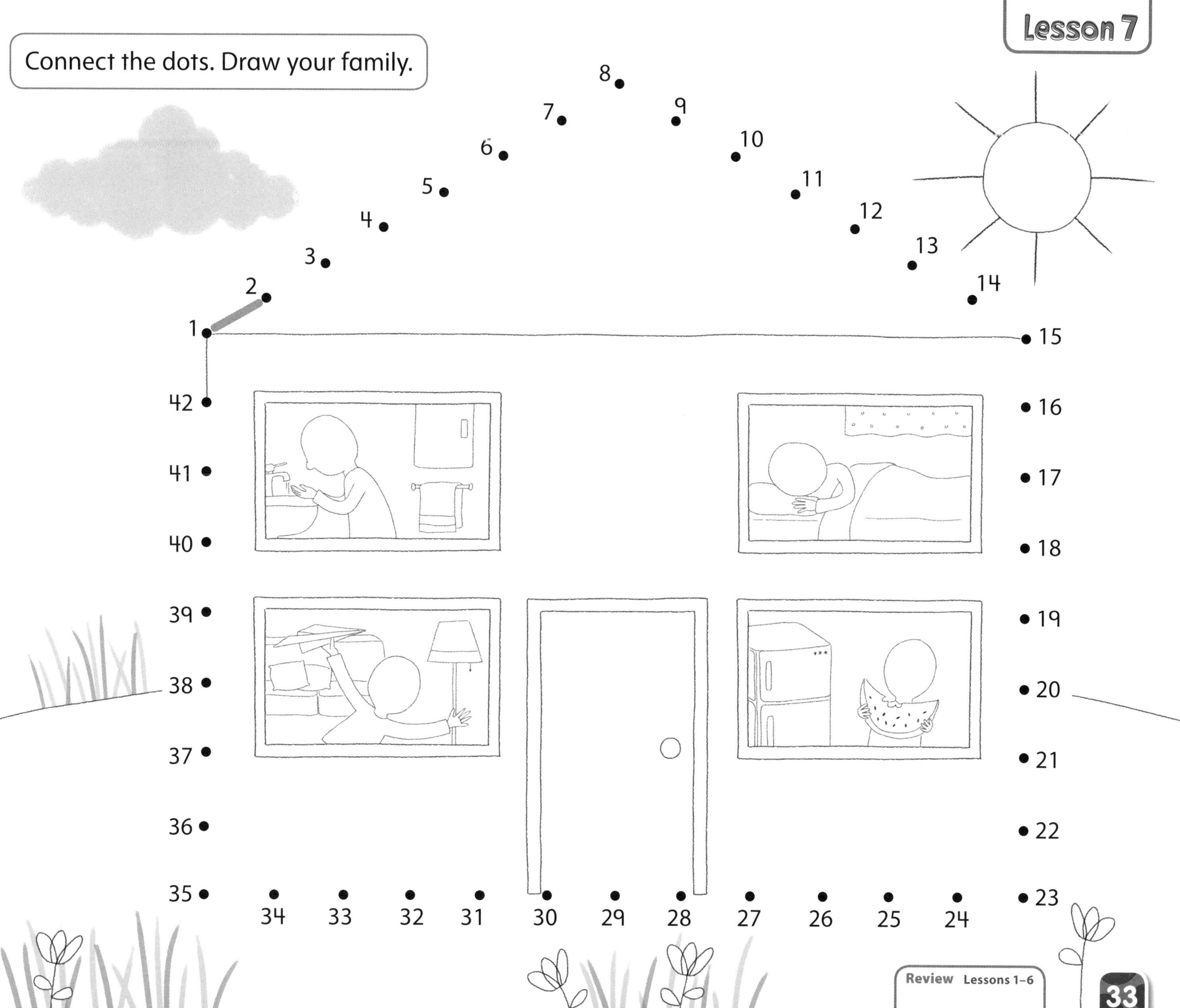
1
2
3
4
5
6
7
8
9
10
11
12
13
14
15
16
17
18
19
20
21
22
23
24
25
26
27
28
29
30
31
32
33
34
35
36
37
38
39
40
41
42

Look and match.

playground

coatroom

classroom

Kindergarten DVD **Kindergarten places**
Vocabulary: *playground, coatroom, classroom*

Trace and write.

door roof wall window

Here is the …

window

__oor

__all

roo__

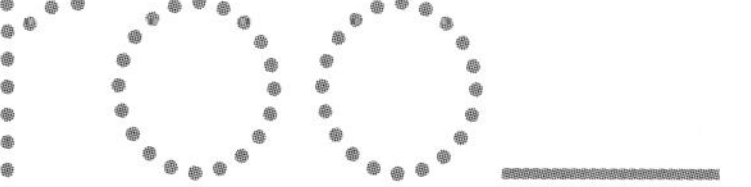

Literacy Writing initial and final letters; tracing partial words
Vocabulary: parts of a house

Follow the numbers.

50
54
51
57
56
52
55
59
53
54
55
55
59
53
56
57
58
59

Numeracy **New numbers:** 50, 51, 52, 53, 54, 55, 56, 57, 58, and 59
Counting

Match and color.

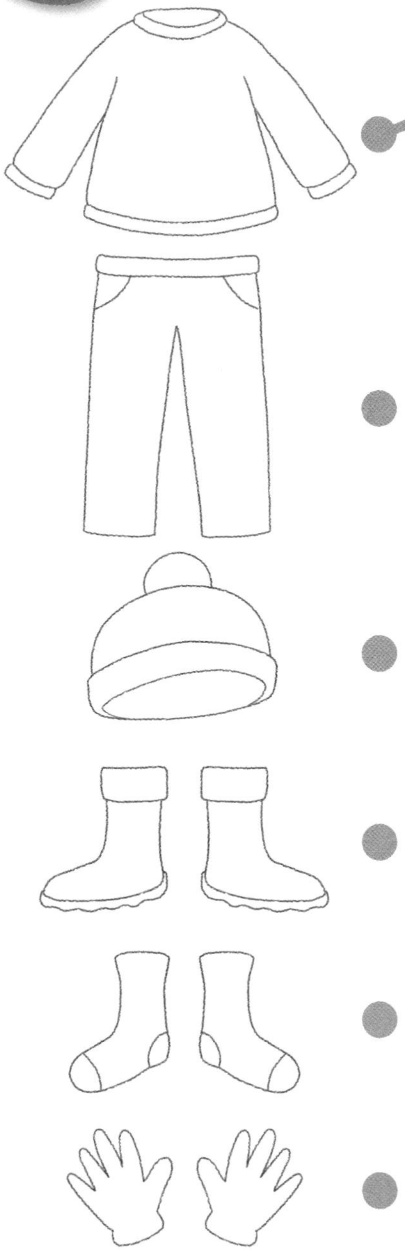

pants

sweater

socks

gloves

boots

hat

New words
Vocabulary: *sweater, pants, hat, boots, socks, gloves*

Trace and match.

Story **Structure:** *Put on your …*
Vocabulary: clothes

Read and trace. Say *Put on your …*

pants
hat
sweater
gloves
socks
boots

Match and color.

winter

spring

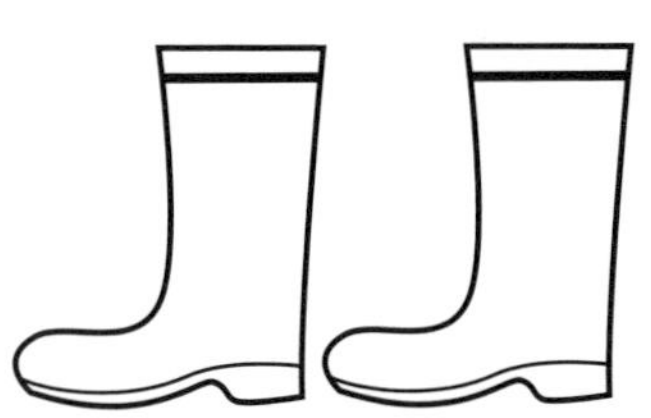

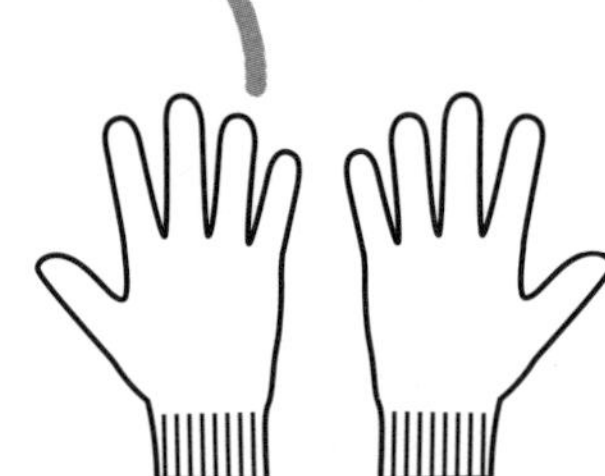

summer

fall

Smart topic Seasons
Vocabulary: *winter, spring, summer, fall*

Draw yourself and your clothes.

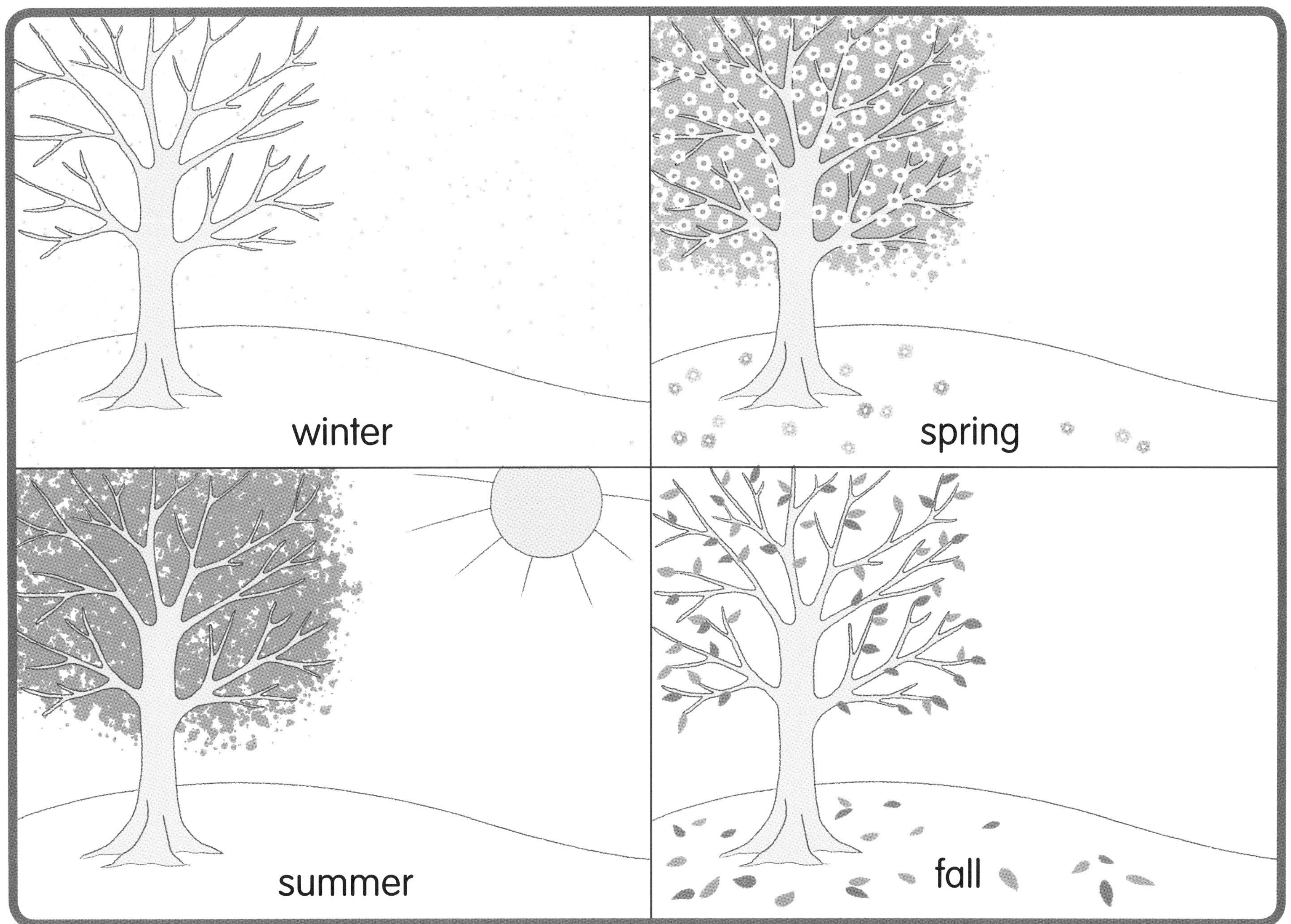
winter
spring
summer
fall

Circle your favorite season. Match.

Seasons

winter

spring

summer

fall

sweater

hat

socks

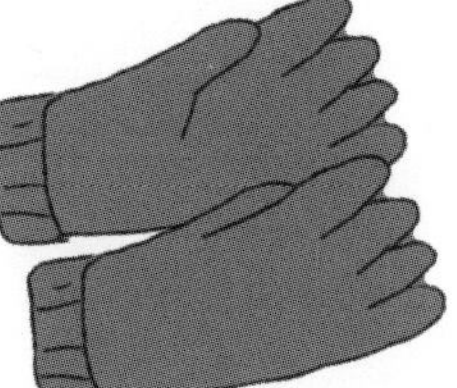

gloves

boots

pants

Look and match.

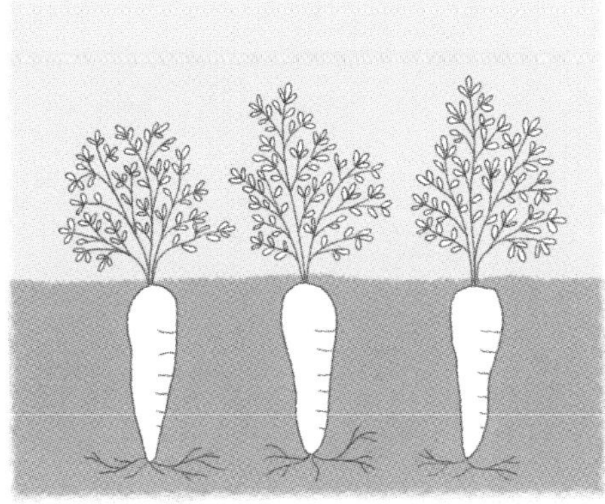

carrots

potatoes

tomatoes

green beans

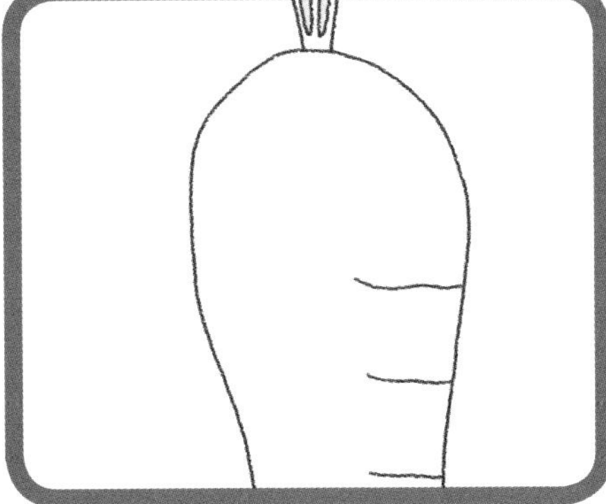

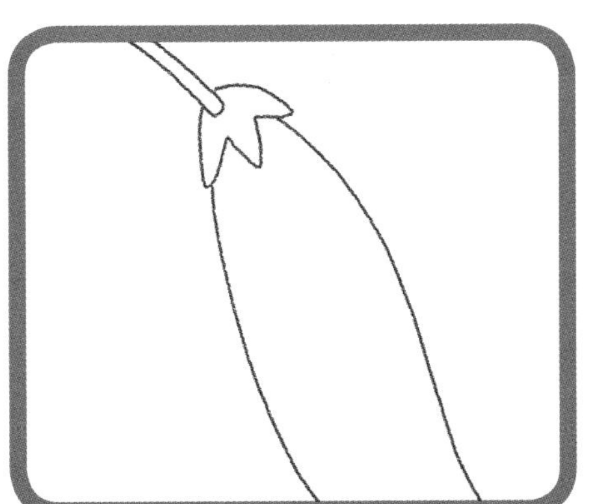

Read and trace. Write.

spring

summer

fall

1
It's fall.

2
It's ________.

3
It's ________.

Literacy Writing whole words
Vocabulary: seasons

Read and color.

60
61
62
63
64
65
66
67
68
69

60 black
61 yellow
62 blue
63 orange
64 pink
65 white
66 purple
67 brown
68 gray
69 green

Numeracy **New numbers:** 60, 61, 62, 63, 64, 65, 66, 67, 68, and 69
Number recognition

Unit 6

Match and color.

seahorse

fish

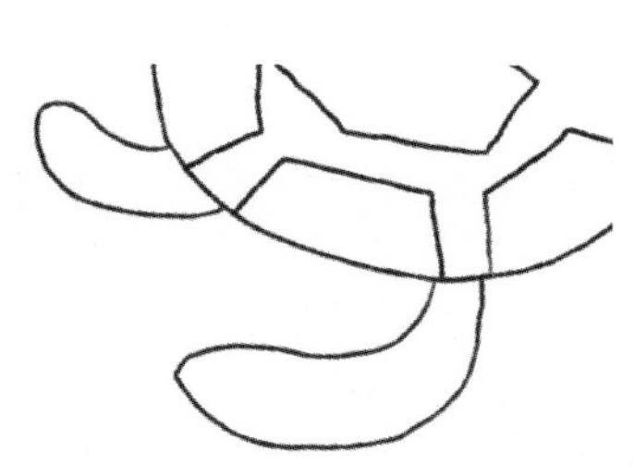

turtle

shark

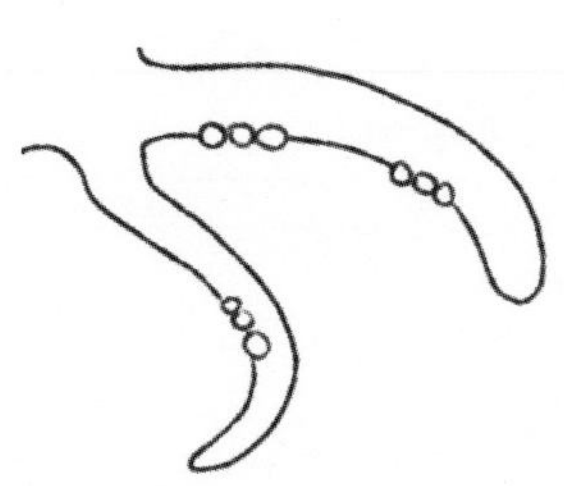

octopus

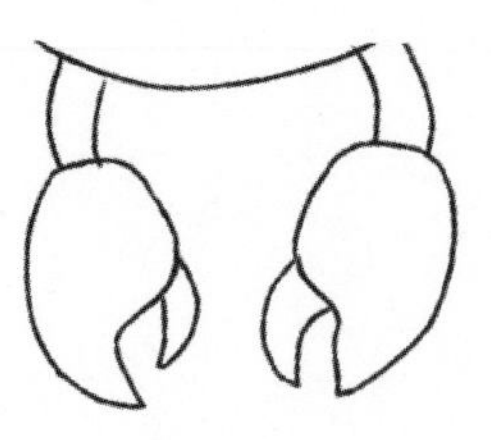

crab

New words
Vocabulary: *turtle, fish, seahorse, shark, octopus, crab*

Remember. Look and ✔ or ✘.

turtle ✔

elephant ✘

fish

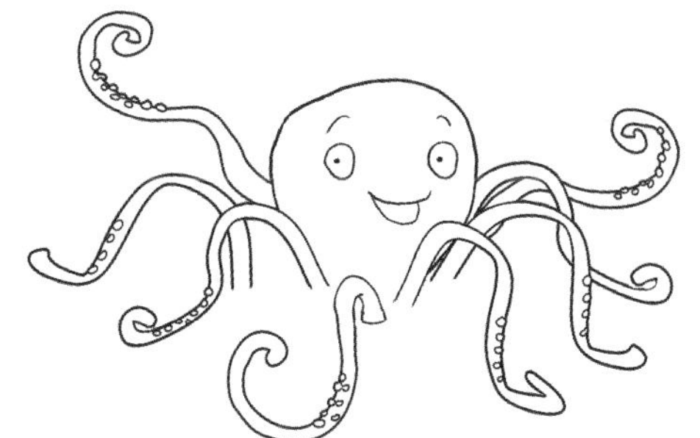

octopus

seahorse

snake

monkey

crab

shark

Read and color. Say *There's a/an …*

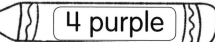

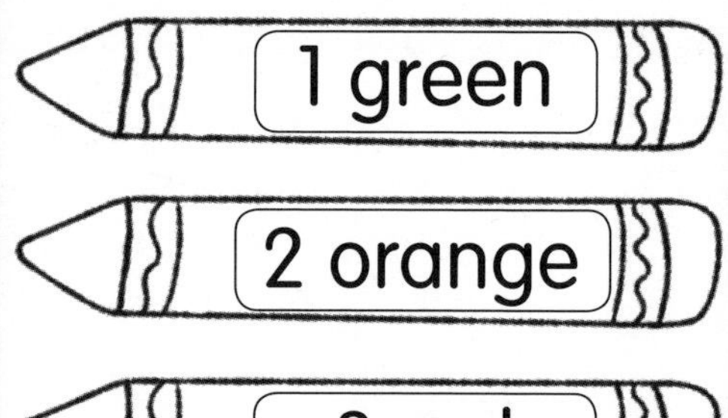

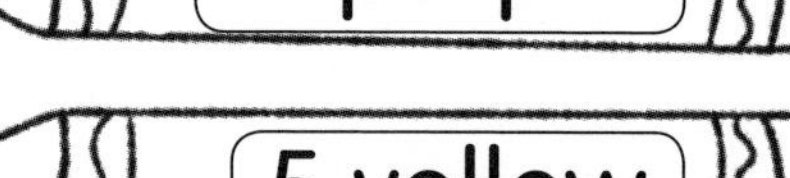

1 green
2 orange
3 red
4 purple
5 yellow
6 gray

2

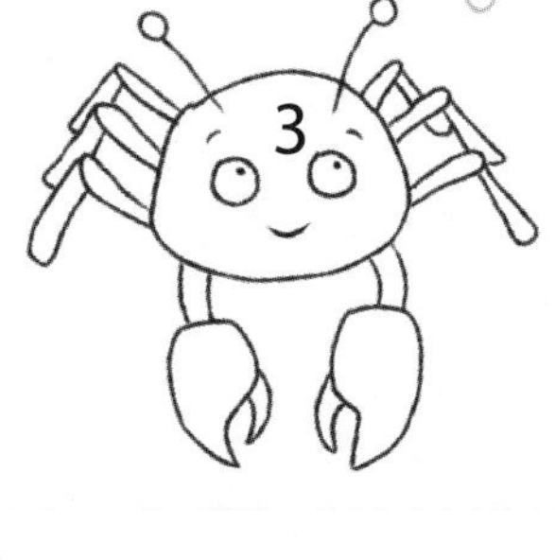
3

1

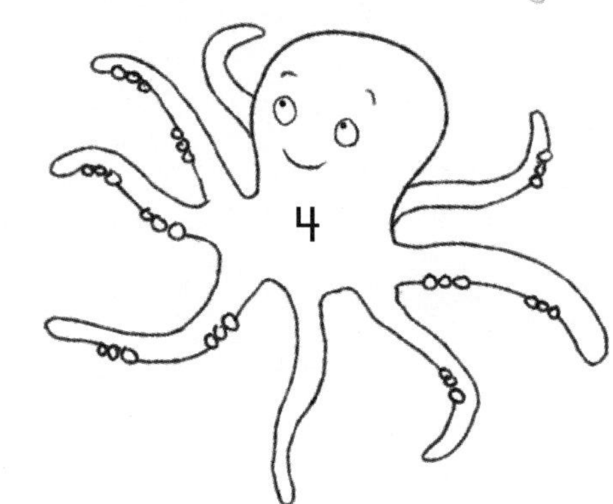
4

5

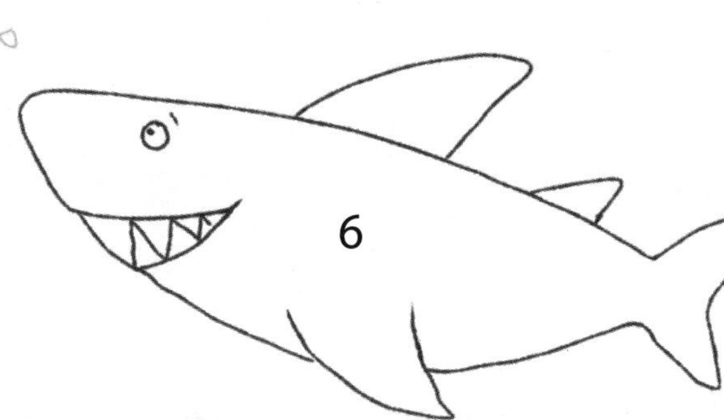
6

Story **Structure:** *There's a/an …*
Vocabulary: sea creatures

Count and write.

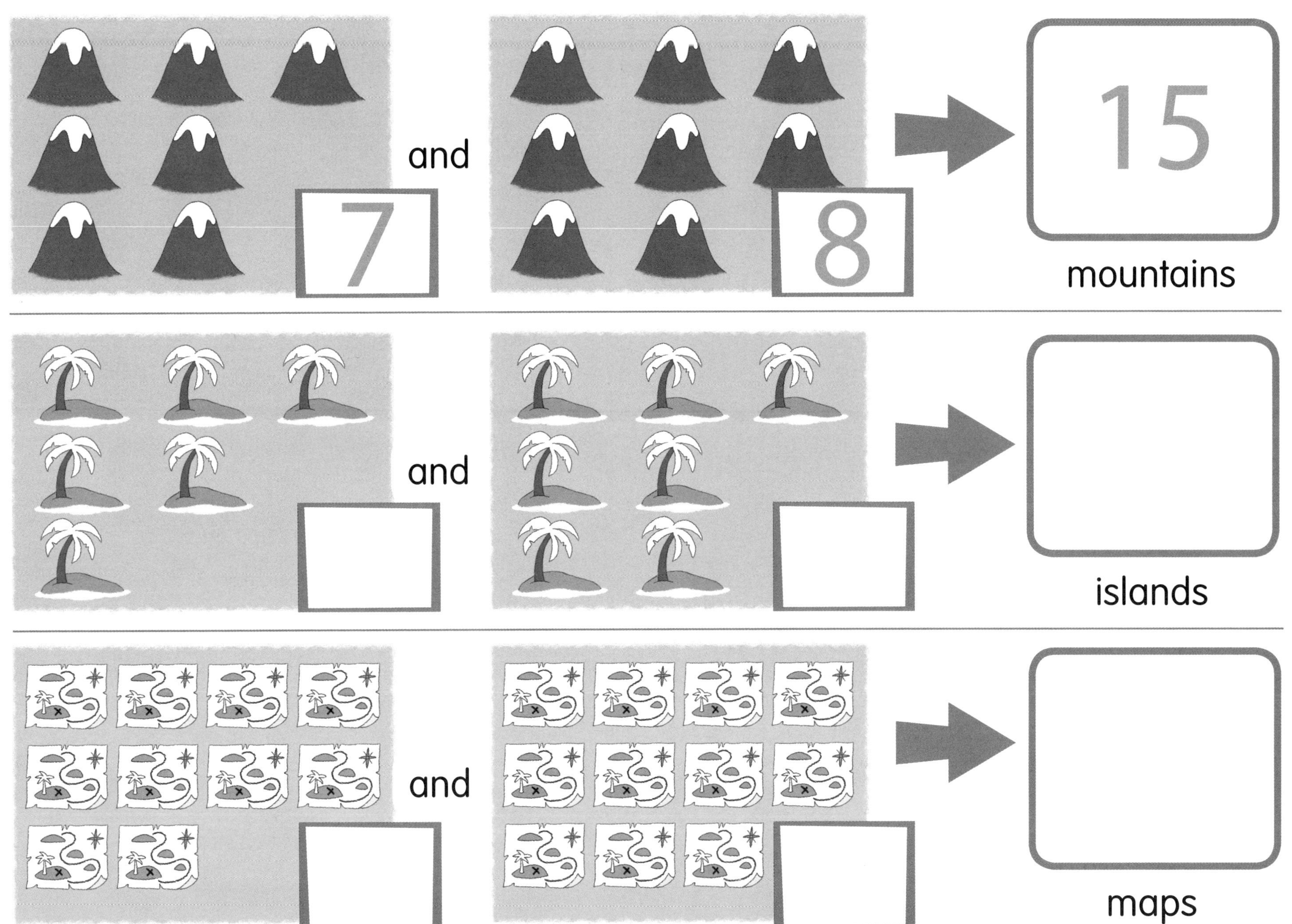
and
7
8
15
mountains
and
islands
and
maps

Smart topic Maps
Vocabulary: *map, island, mountain, beach*

Look and circle 6 differences in Picture 2.

1

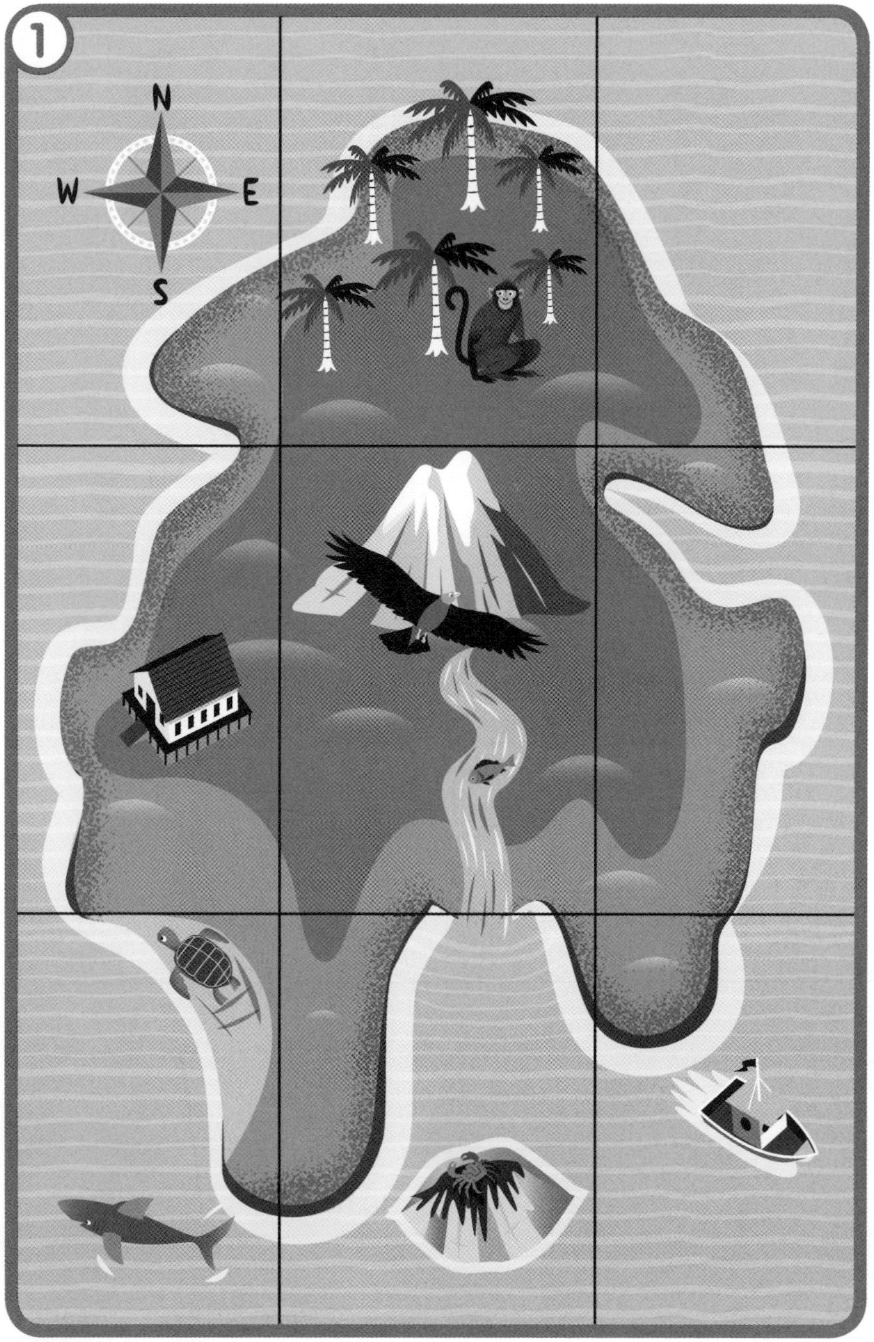

N
W
E
S

2

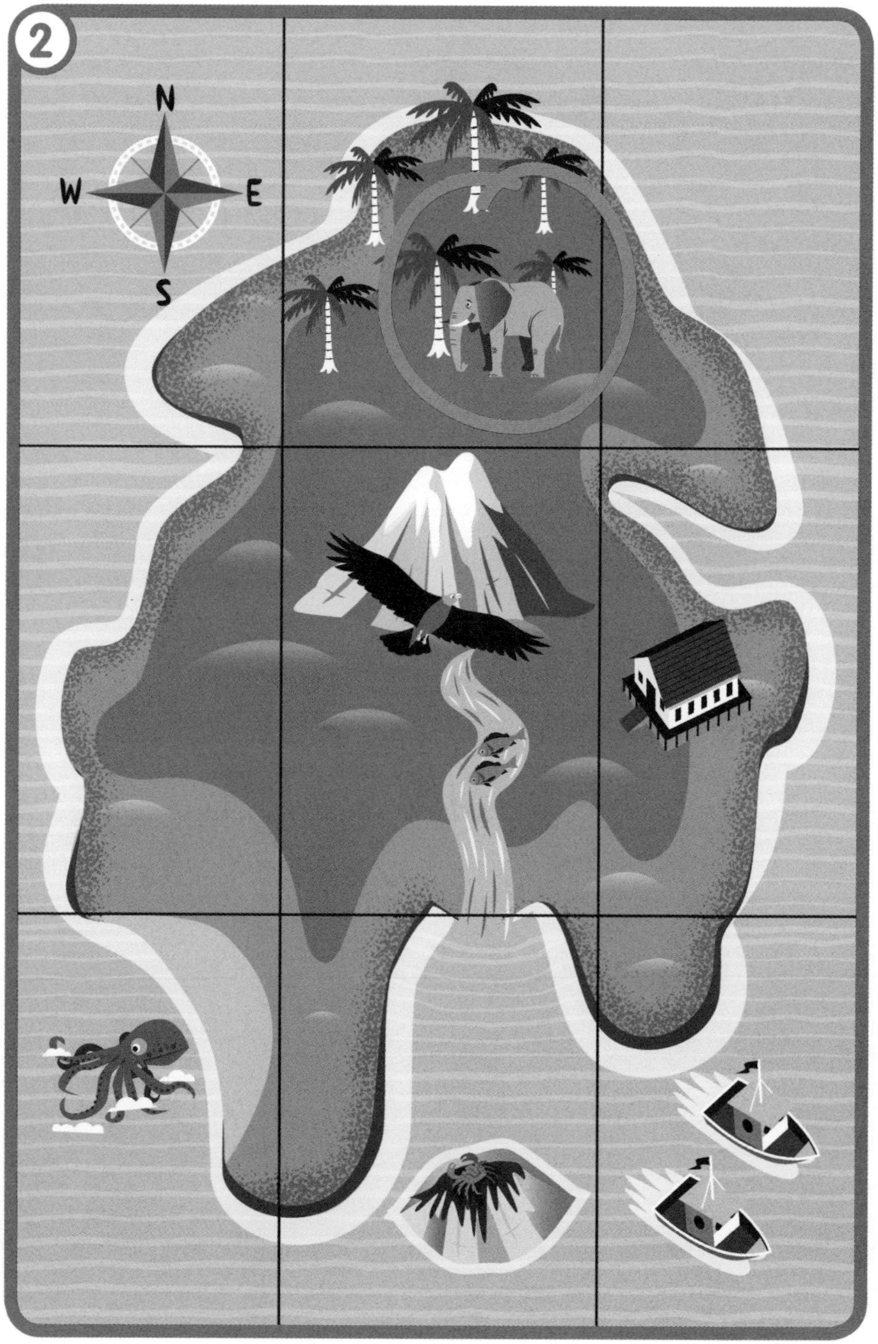

N
W
E
S

Draw yourself. Circle your favorite sea creature.

Look and draw.

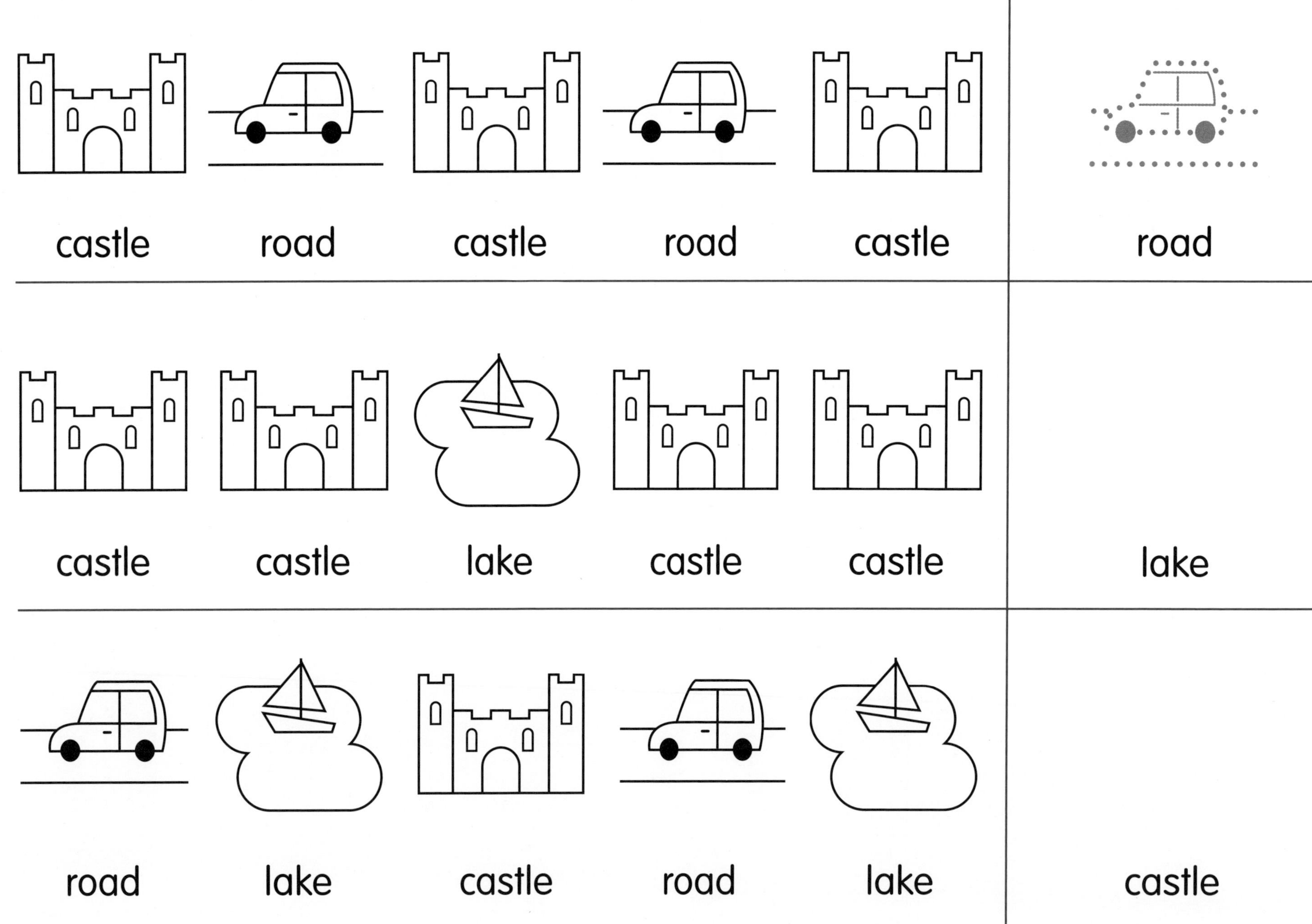
castle
road
castle
road
castle
road
castle
castle
lake
castle
castle
lake
road
lake
castle
road
lake
castle

Kindergarten DVD **Sand play**
Vocabulary: *castle, road, lake*

Trace and read. Write.

island castle crab

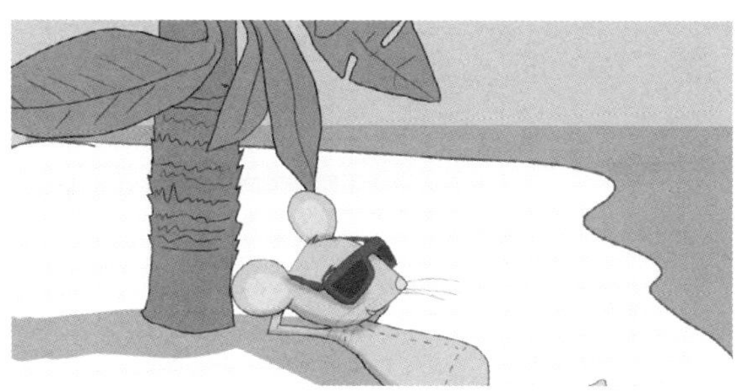

There's an island.

There's a .

There's a .

Literacy Writing whole words
Vocabulary: *castle, crab, island*

Connect the dots.

25 26 27 24 28 23 29 22 30 8 9 21 19 18 7 10 20 17 13 14 15 12 31 16 11 6 32 5 4 3 33 2 34 1 35 38 37 39 36 40 77 41 76 78 42 79 75 43 49 48 71 47 74 72 70 50 44 73 46 45 69 68 51 63 64 65 53 52 67 62 66 54 61 55 60 56 59 58 57

Numeracy **New numbers:** 70, 71, 72, 73, 74, 75, 76, 77, 78, and 79
Counting

Unit
7

Look and match.

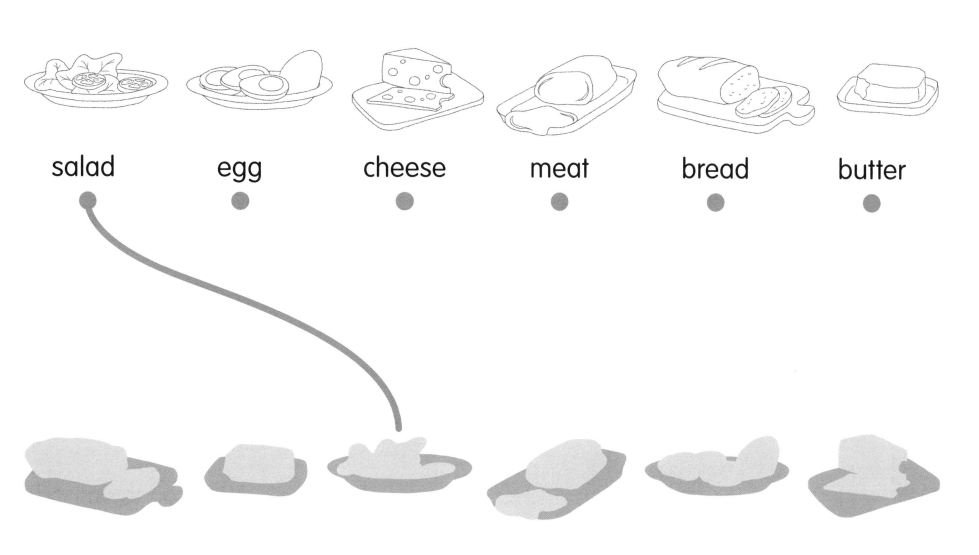

salad egg cheese meat bread butter

New words
Vocabulary: *bread, cheese, butter, meat, egg, salad*

Remember. Number in order.

Salad and egg, please.

Meat and cheese, please.

1

Bread, please.

Mmm!

Butter, please.

Lunch!

Story **Structure:** *Give me the …, please.*
Vocabulary: food

Read and draw. Circle for your sandwich. Say *Give me the …, please.*

bread

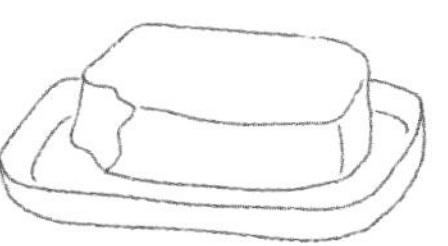

butter

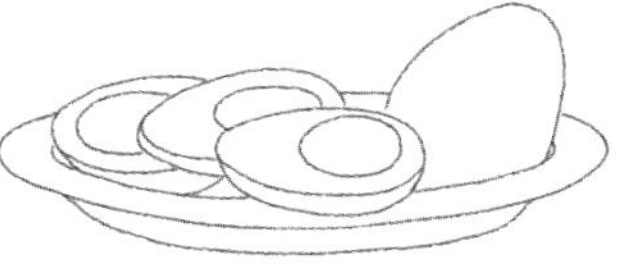

egg

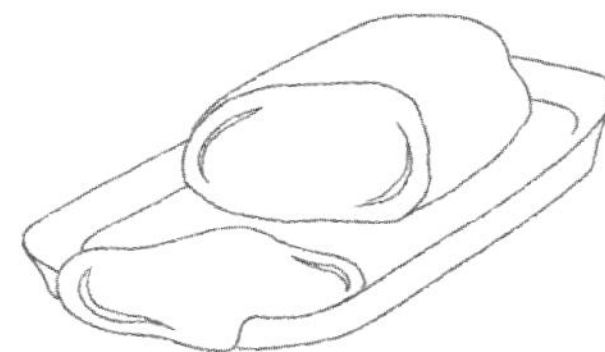

meat

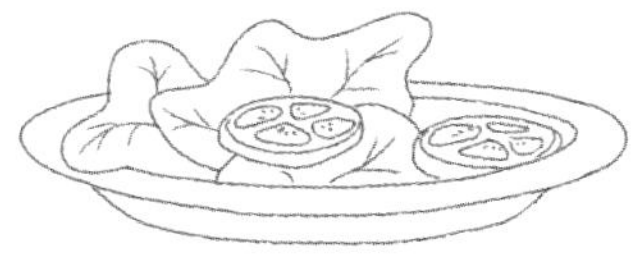

salad

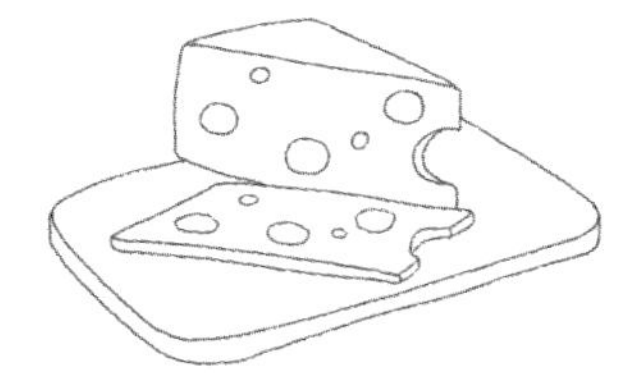

cheese

Follow and draw.

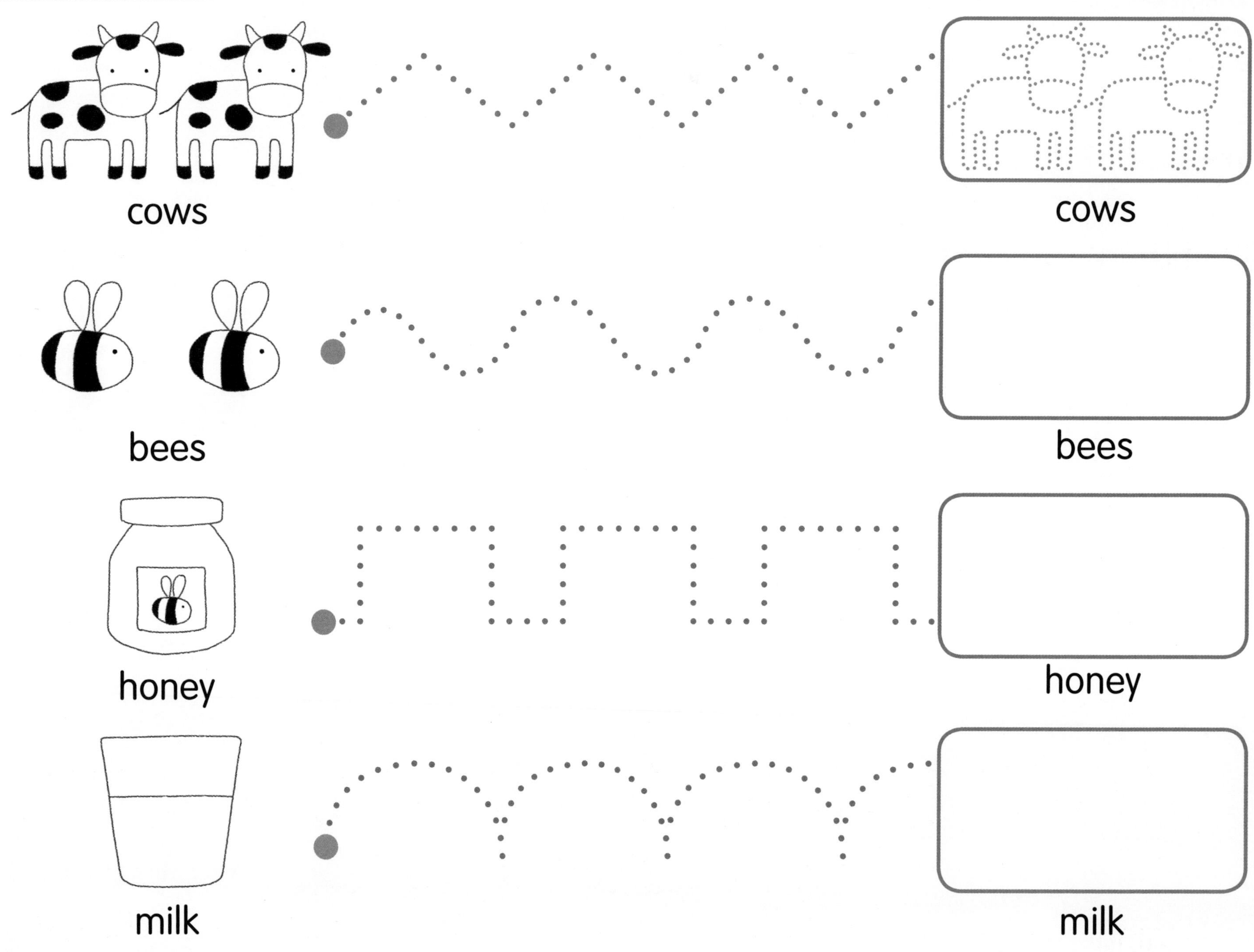
cows
cows
bees
bees
honey
honey
milk
milk

Smart topic **Food from animals**
Vocabulary: *chickens, bees, cows, eggs, honey, milk*

Count and write the number.

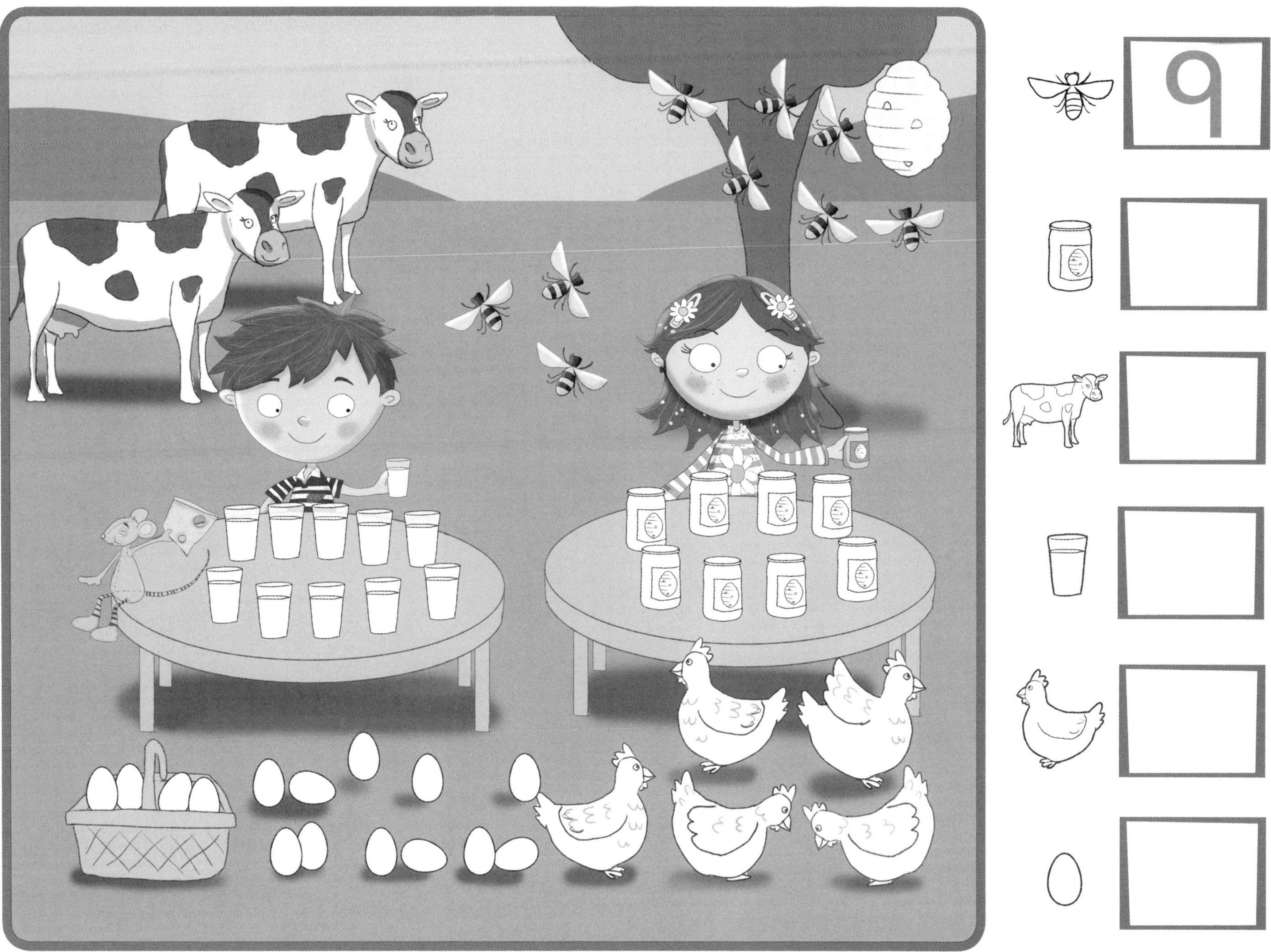

9

Do you like it? Look and ✔ or ✘.

salad ☐

eggs ☐

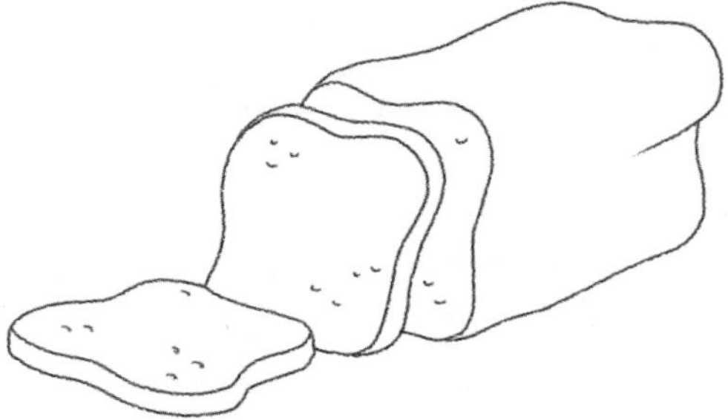

bread 

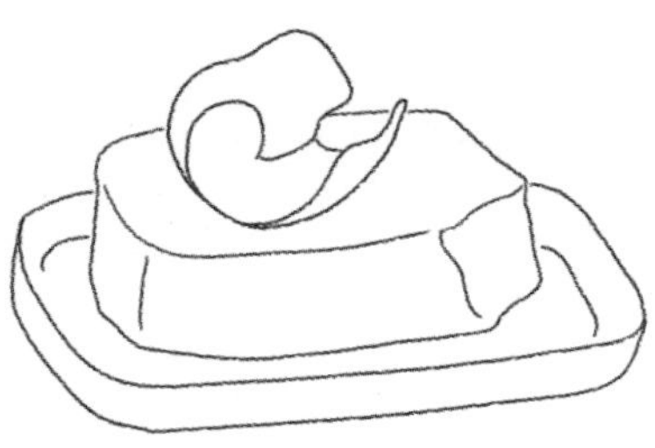

butter ☐

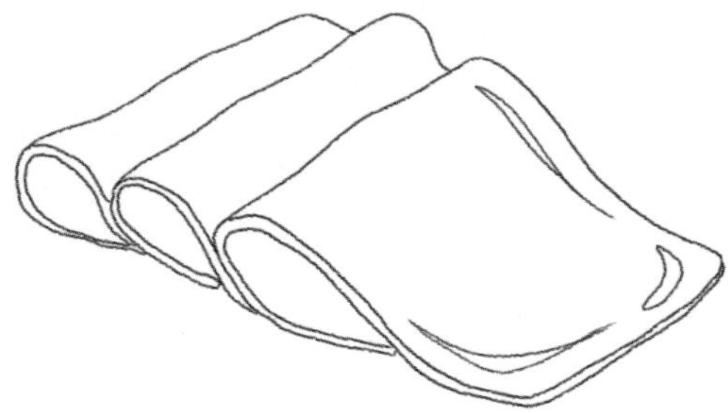

meat ☐

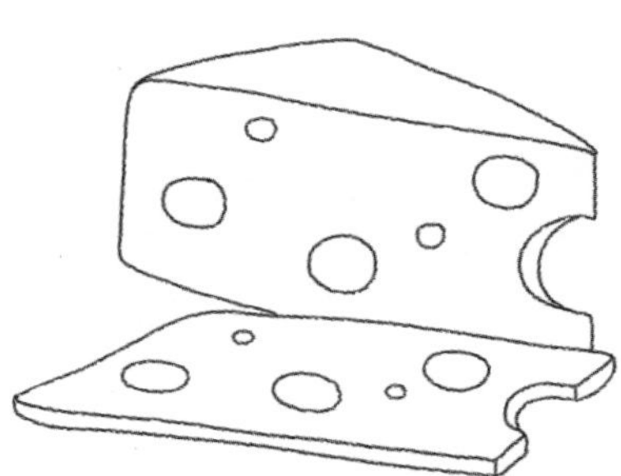

cheese ☐

honey 

milk ☐

Look and circle the one that is the same.

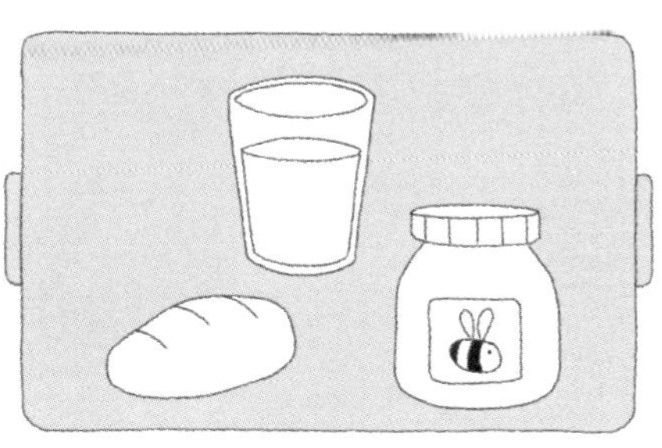

breakfast

snack

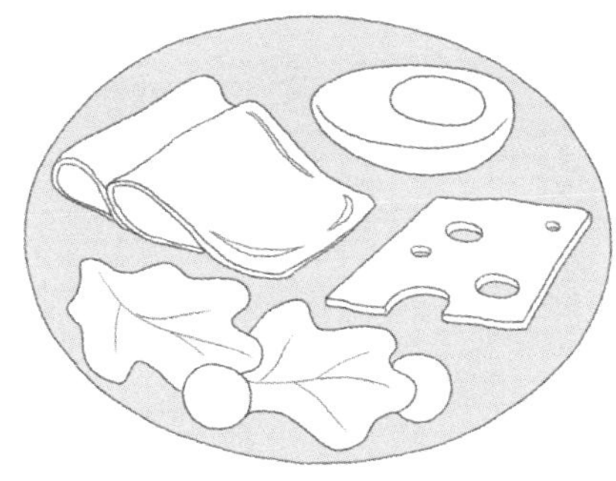
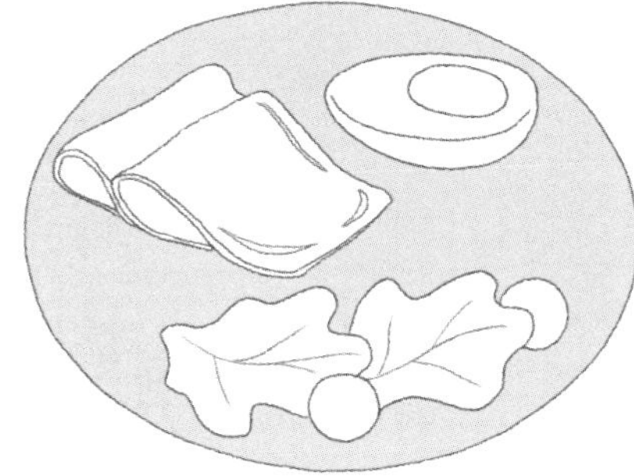

lunch

Read and write.

Eggs cows Honey cows

Butter comes from cows.

__________ comes from bees.

__________ come from chickens.

Milk comes from __________ .

Literacy Writing whole words
Vocabulary: *eggs, honey, cows*

Write the next number.

78 

86 

84 

83 

80 

88 

85 

87 

82 

81 

79 

77 

Trace and color.

leaves
bench
pond
grass
path
flowers

New words
Vocabulary: *pond, grass, path, leaves, flowers, bench*

Look and circle 6 differences in Picture 2.

1

2

Read and trace. Say *in* or *on*.

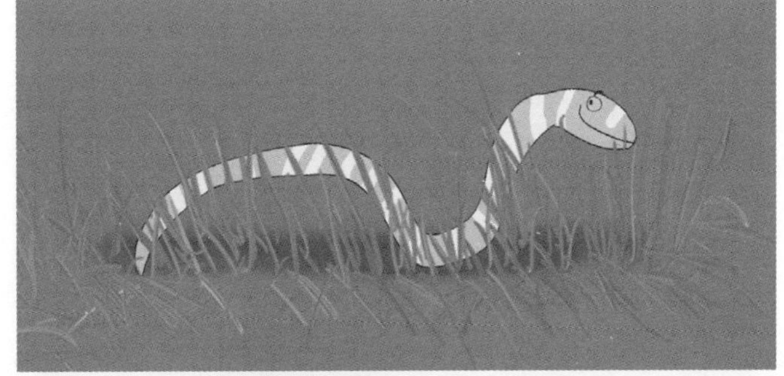

in the grass

on the path

on the bench

in the park

Trace and write the number. Color.

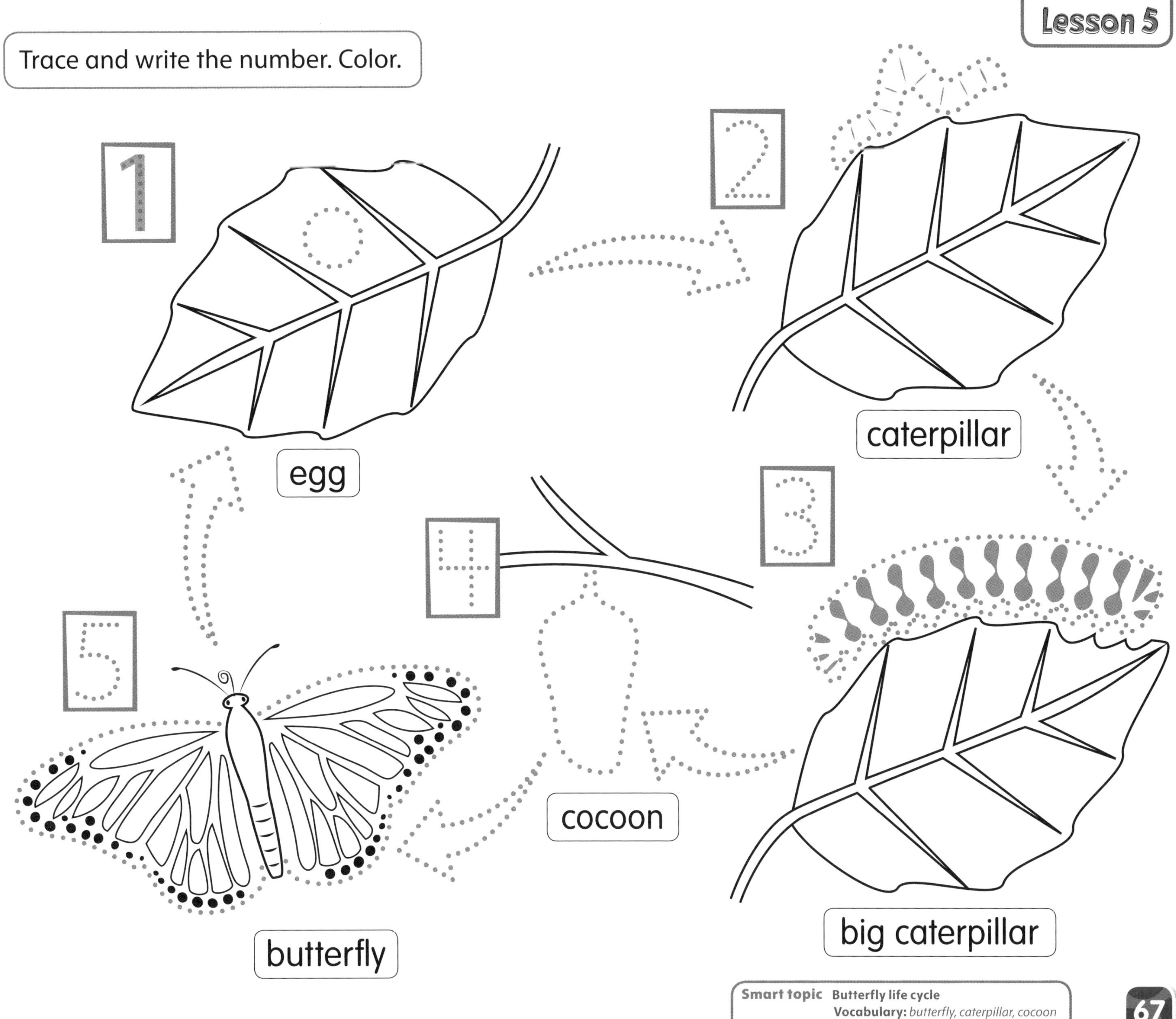
1
2
3
4
5
egg
caterpillar
big caterpillar
cocoon
butterfly

Smart topic Butterfly life cycle
Vocabulary: *butterfly, caterpillar, cocoon*

Look and color.

○ green △ orange □ black

Look, circle, and ✔.

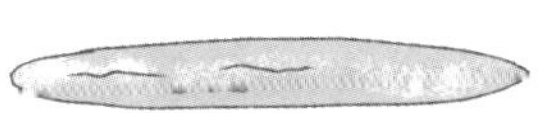

pond 

leaves ☐

grass ☐

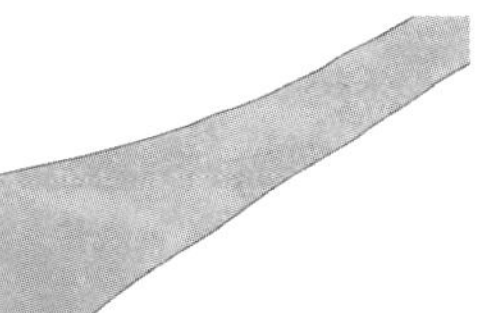

path ☐

butterfly ☐

flowers ☐

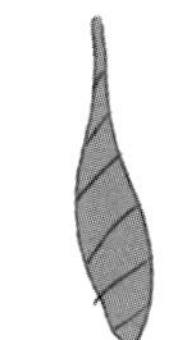

cocoon ☐

bird ☐

69

Look and circle the one that is different.

ladybug

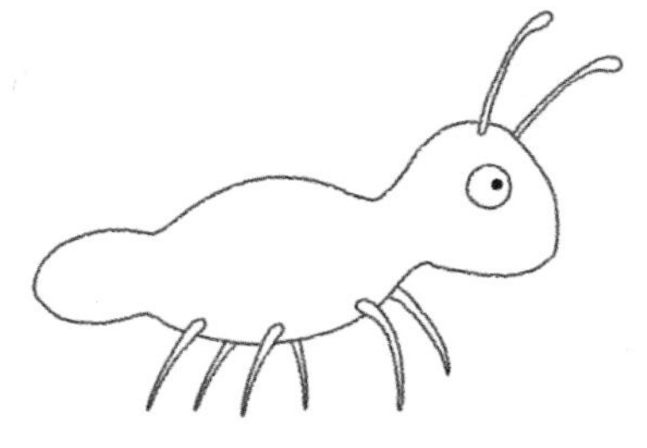

ant

spider

Trace, read, and color. Read and circle.

1
green

2
yellow

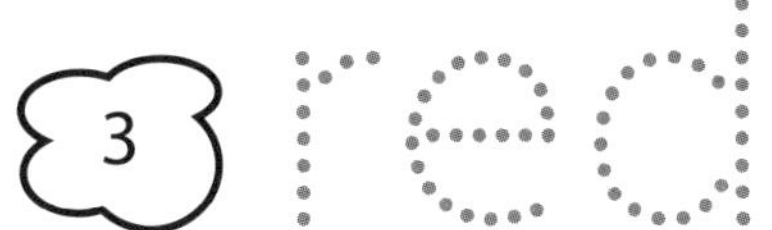
3
red

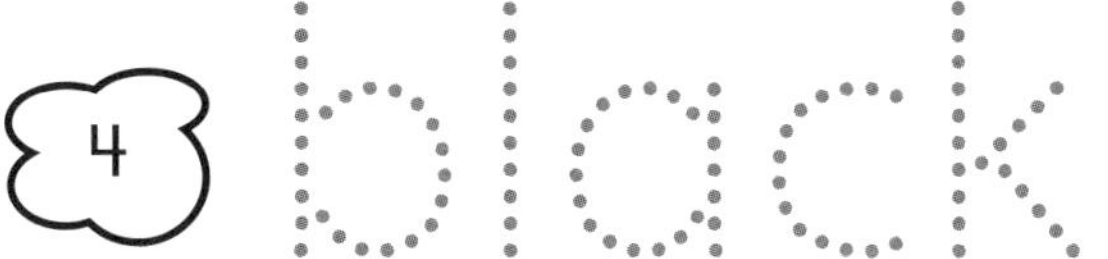
4
black

5
brown

The flowers are red.	Yes	No	The grass is green.	Yes	No
The butterfly is orange.	Yes	No	The spider is brown.	Yes	No

Follow the numbers.

30
100
20
40
10
60
50
90
70
60
80
50
70
80
90
100
60

Numeracy **New numbers**: 90, 91, 92, 93, 94, 95, 96, 97, 98, 99, and 100
Counting